About tl

Nigel Wilson breaking away in the British Professional Road Race Championships 2003

Nigel Wilson was born in Sheffield (1966) with a damaged right ventricular (ARVD). In spite of this and thanks to his father's gentle persuasion, Nigel competitively cycle raced for 22 years, whilst working fulltime - 6 days a week - in his family's cycle shop. During his time as a racing cyclist, he was able to win a series of diverse races, ranging from the locally prestigious "Sheffield City centre race" (1985) to the hellishly, fast and hilly Norfolk Park (Sheffield) circuit race.

His crowning achievement was when he became the Yorkshire 100 mile time trial champion, leading him to become the Peter Greenwood memorial trophy winner in 1989. Which was incorporated into the National 100 mile time trial championships, as the British event was held in Yorkshire that year. And Nigel only entered and raced in that time trial because there was no local road race on that day, riding on his road bike, with his Sheffield Phoenix jersey tucked into his shorts and his cotton cap turned around backwards, finishing only 3 seconds behind Eddie Atkins, a multinational time trial champion and national time trial record holder.

This effort was closely followed by his silver medal in the North Midlands Division road race championship in 1989, which he was able to achieve with no team mates, placing in front of National road race champion Simeon Hempsall and Commonwealth Games bronze medal winner Wayne Randle.

Not too shabby, given that from a very early age Nigel hated cycling. To such an extent that at around the age of 7, in a silent protest against going on the weekly Sunday Sheffield Phoenix club run (cycle ride), Nigel recalls hiding the keys to the house and shop under the living room carpet. This ultimately left his parents key hunting for the day, leaving Nigel to play "innocently" with his toys. Fortunately for Nigel, his father was a very understanding man, where over the years, through a gentle and patient persuasion, he was able to spark the passion he felt for cycling in his son.

Although Nigel did not quite realise it at the time, his father was a cycling genius, and he credits all of his aforementioned accomplishments to his father's inspiration and light handed guidance. But with age and wisdom Nigel has now come to realise the epic depth of his dad's character, prompting him to write this biography on the inspirational life of his father Jim Wilson that he wishes to share with the reader.

To Jim and Olive Wilson, my father and mother, two very special people.

Nigel James Wilson

Jim Wilson: He Hath Courage

A Legend is an Understatement

Austin Macauley Publishers®
London * Cambridge * New York * Sharjah

All of the events in this memoir are true to the best of author's memory. The views expressed in this memoir are solely those of the author.

A CIP catalogue record for this title is available from the British Library.

ISBN 9781035886708 (Paperback)
ISBN 9781035886715 (ePub e-book)

www.austinmacauley.com

First Published 2026
Austin Macauley Publishers Ltd®
1 Canada Square
Canary Wharf
London
E14 5AA

Thank you to all the people mentioned in this book and elsewhere, who passed on their fond memories of my father, and the life inspiring stories that Jim related to them.

Table of Contents

Lemonade and Turnips	**25**
A View from a Hill	**27**
Chocolate Canary	**29**
UXB	**31**
Impact	**34**
Doing His Best	**36**
Boot Loot	**37**
Paper Millionaires	**39**
A Wall Away	**41**
Blonde Tuft	**42**
Black Bull	**43**
German Warm Water Torture	**44**
Caught Short	**77**
Incident of Indecent Exposure	**78**
KKK	**89**
Epilogue	**90**

Over the years, many people have said to me that I should write a book about my father or, having listened to me speak with such a passion of various parts of his life, have asked me whether I have already written a book about his life! And I have always smiled and shook my head and humorously thought to myself:

No, because it would take a Shakespeare to do Jim Wilson justice.

But having considered this, I now realise that if anything is to be related about Mr JF Wilson, (lovingly known to everyone as Jim), that it is down to me to do so. It has become obvious that no one else would be able to write an apposite biography about my father no matter how gifted they were. And in the kind of world that we live in today, why should they want to? Without any media attention, Mozart would be an also-ran.

Even after having lived and worked with my father for a good 28 years, I feel that this book is only the tip of a very large, story-filled iceberg. Jim was soft-spoken and did not push conversations (or anything else) onto you. You pleased yourself whether you listened or not. This in itself was attractive and endearing. I know, I for one listened, and I am very pleased that I was there in those circumstances with an inclination to do so.

*

One of my first memories of Jim was cycling with him on the back of his bike towards Rivelin Reservoir, on the road to Moscar in Derbyshire, along with my Mum Olive, Jim's wife, one Sunday morning. What a wonderful ride it was, there in the lovely fresh air, as we cycled up the quiet Rivelin Valley road, under the dappling shade of lovely, big, leafy trees that greeted us on both sides of the snaking and undulating road for well over a mile! I was seated on a child's seat that Jim had built and fitted onto the back of his racing, touring and clubman's road bike—he always made do with one bike—the one that he had raced on in the first ever Tour of Britain in 1951, (and even before that) and the one he had raced on in the next three following Tours of Britain, along with Classic races on the continent and everything else that could be raced in at home and abroad. A bike with a steel frame and forks that, as a master cycle frame builder, he had also personally hand-built, brazing them together, using some of the greatest steel tubing the world has ever produced, both very strong and perfectly light. A frame and forks that Jim would assemble into a world-class, hand-built bike, a bike also known as a *JF Wilson*.

For safety, the chair was fitted with little, white leather seatbelt straps. (I remember the seat, but don't recall the straps, but there they are on a photo from that period), although we wore no cycle helmets; after all, this was 1969.

There is a photo of me (a year or two older after losing my dummy) and Jim with Jim's bike and seat, taken by Olive around the other side of Rivelin Reservoir from the viaduct.

Also there is another photo of myself, again a few years later on, on the back of a tandem bike that my mother Olive is riding, with Jim following on his bike on the same Moscar road, that a lady called Rene Cason (From Zetland, Doncaster. Happily, the person's name and details are written on the back of the photo) took as we passed by, who caught us up in her car and let my parents know that she had taken a photo of us, and if they gave her our address she would send it to us…those were the days…. who would bother or even think that they had the time to do that today? Who would dare, out of kindness, these days, to take a photo of someone's family and then follow them and ask them for their address?

Photo of me (the author) a year or two older after losing my dummy and Jim with Jim's bike and seat, taken by Olive around the other side of Rivelin Reservoir from the Viaduct.

Jim and Olive, with me literally *in* tandem, are going up the Rivelin Valley Road, having set off from our home and cycle shop on City Road in Sheffield. I'm two or three years old, and every now and then, Olive rides up alongside us as we enjoy life, the good weather and the countryside together.

Another photo of myself, again a few years later on, on the back of a tandem bike that my mother Olive is riding with Jim following on his bike on the Moscar Road, that a lady called Rene Cason took.

We stop off at Rivelin Reservoir to take a look at the beautiful water-filled dam before we continue on our journey to Castleton, and a little café there, that I recall for selling large, homemade ginger biscuits.

- Or maybe on that day, it was just to go about a quarter of a mile, up the road, around a few bends from the entrance and viaduct of Rivelin Dam to a cosy, little, wooden shack of a café, that greeted us, from its nestling foliaged position, on the gradual upward slope of the road. I fondly remember this little oasis, for their two Jack Russell dogs, the smell of old mugs of tea and real chocolate and jam wagon wheel biscuits, individually wrapped in their paper packets. In the days before our treats became over sweetened casino chips.

The author in the village of Baslow, Derbyshire. Quite a bike ride from Sheffield, for a 5 or 6 year old with 16" wheels and a single gear, even on a hand built J.F. Wilson 531 frame with Nervex lugs.

Mum, Olive outside The Cabin Café on Moscar; the bike is a J.F. Wilson of course

But before we potter along the narrow reservoir road to view the dam properly, we have a look over the railings of the viaduct that we have stopped on, just off the main road, down in to the little side tributary. And whilst I was in my mum's arms, looking over the top of the railings, I remember my dummy falling down from out of my mouth, and landing by the side of the open culvert's briskly flowing central stream, that runs down the dam's concrete spillway.

And thinking even then, as my dummy lay inches away from being washed away: we are lucky that on this day the stream is not a torrent. Crying out at that, I became aware—calmed with alarm and wonder—when Jim, perhaps driven by the thought of me crying for the rest of the day without my comforter, climbed over the iron palings of the bridge, walked along the grassy top banking on our right, to the channel's wall, that can still be seen today as being around 20 feet deep, with, at about halfway down its face, the end of a water pipe sticking out approximately six inches from the stone wall's vertical surface.

Standing two inches over six feet, Jim hung from the top of the wall by his fingers and managed to stand (in cycling shoes or bare feet? Take your pick) on the curvature of the pipe that had a diameter no larger than a medium-sized melon. And letting go at the top of the wall, whilst holding himself against the wall's face to maintain his balance on the end of the pipe, he then somehow (I must have turned, or have been turned away at this dangerous moment) bent down at the knees to hold onto the pipe. And hanging from the pipe at arms' length, dropped the rest of the way down to the sloping concrete floor below. My dummy was retrieved from the side of the stream and returned, and Jim became more than a Tarzan to me from then on. By the way, Jim was 50 years old when he made that impromptu descent for my dummy.

Looking back, now that I' am of a similar age to Jim, (52 at the time of writing) the memory speaks volumes. At three years old, I did not know much about age. Yet I was still nevertheless impressed, and this is one of the reasons why I have cherished this memory throughout my life.

It impressed me partly because I realised even then that I had witnessed a feat, by someone I love and care for, putting themselves at risk for me, someone they love and care for. Eventually, the day came when Olive told me that she had sent my dummy to the Moon; and perhaps it was then that my interest in astronomy began.

Jim seemed to be from an older generation than Olive, probably because he had married quite late in life, when he was 39 years old and when Olive was 24 years of age. Or to put it into perspective, when Jim was 20 years old and fighting in World War 2, Olive was five years old and a tot at nursery; such are the fates of life. For the record, they were married on Boxing Day, the Christmas of 1958, at St Christopher's Church in Shiregreen, Sheffield.

Before they were married, Jim had asked Olive if she would like an engagement ring or a bike. Olive chose the bike, but years later, she jokingly said she must have been mad, as she would have been given the bike anyway.

They honeymooned at Blackpool, and when they arrived at their boarding house, they realised that neither of them had brought any money, each thinking that the other would have brought some with them. During my life, I rarely saw Jim using a telephone, but on this occasion, I was told that he did, to ask his mother in Sheffield to organise and send some money over to Blackpool.

It was not until much later in my life that these true stories, that have pleasantly haunted mine and my mother's memories and lives, have now been passed on to you dear reader to hopefully enjoy and share.

So for love, not necessarily for money, here goes.

James Fredrick Wilson was born and bred in Sheffield—the world's capital of Steel—on the 27th of July 1919.

Originating from the then-hardworking Pitsmoor area of Sheffield and moving during his formative years to the then-newly built Southy Green estate.

Jim's father was in the horse cavalry during the First World War, and after the war worked in the Steel works (Not on piece work). And Jim followed suit, having been given his father's tools at the age of 14. Working in various steel works around Sheffield and earning the nick name Lofty. But Lofty began to dislike the working conditions and often looked up at the skylights and longed to be outside. So at around the age of 18, Jim joined the army to escape.

Stationed in Kirkcudbright in Scotland Jim said that the local people were the kindest people that he had ever met. And on Christmas Day all the young soldiers were invited to their dinners with local families. And also to dances and other local entertainments during the festive season.

The 26th Field Company. Jim Wilson, also known then as "Lofty" is 2nd from the reader's right on the back row

The army was not keen on Jim's love of cycling, and he would be picked up by the military police for going too far away and put in the slammer. Until Jim won a cross-country running race, where a card had to be stamped at different checkpoints around the course. The race officials did not believe it at first when Jim handed in his card first, presuming that he had cut the race route short—as some of the competitors did who had called it a day—and as they were expecting one of their favourites: "All the gear, no idea" runners to win. But there it was. Proof! They wanted Jim to join the running team, but he showed them his bruised black toenails and said he was not a runner but a cyclist.

On leave, Jim would cycle ride from Kirkcudbrightshire in Southwest Scotland to Sheffield in South Yorkshire, to see his family and friends. And then cycle the return journey, hoping that the army officials would be none the wiser—after all they did not want him straying too far!

On one occasion up in Scotland, they took the men out in the back of a covered army lorry and scattered them into the middle of the middle of nowhere, for them to try to survive and find their own way back. Some of them were lost for days. Jim and his friend found a road the same day, and caught a lift off a passing baker's lorry, eating cakes in the back all the way back to the barracks.

Jim soon turned Catholic after joining the army. The Christian soldiers on a Sunday had to march up and down a square for most of the day. Whereas the Catholic soldiers went to mass in the morning and then had the rest of the day to themselves.

Any of the courses that were going in the army, Jim took them. He was not one for sitting around in the barracks smoking and playing cards. By the end of it, he could speak German fluently, diffuse mines, was very athletic and was trained to build Bailey bridges and blow bridges up. For a young man, all this seemed much better than working in the steel works, and he soon built up an impressive CV. Which backfired on him because when the Second World War broke out, guess whose name was at the top of the list?

From the age of 20, initially starting out with the 26th Field Company, Jim served six years in the Second World War, as a sapper in the Royal Engineers. Jim always said that physically these six years were the best years of his life, and were regrettably lost to his favourite sport of cycle racing. And I have often thought that Fausto Coppi, Lousin Bobet and Rick Van Steenbergen et al were the luckier for that.

Jim Winning the prime at the top of the Shap in the Tour of Britain. Not a bad climber for 6 foot 2, especially after bowel surgery the previous year.

Consider for a moment, Fausto Coppi—one of the most famous professional road racing cyclist Italy has ever produced, and in accordance was looked after and highly respected by his nation—was captured, after surrendering to the British army, and ended up cutting soldiers' hair during the rest of WW2 in a POW camp. Whilst Jim Wilson was enduring the full, life shortening hardships of war, blowing up bridges in FRONT of the front line, to slow down the German advance on Dunkirk.

My father had to have part of his bowel removed in 1950, from having to drink and eat dirty water and food during the six years of the war, as well as suffering with shell shock for two years directly after the war. And remember that Jim was no spring chicken in all of these post war stories, for example, at the time of the inaugural Tour of Britain in 1951 Jim was already 32 years old, and by the time of the Coppi race on the Isle of Man he was nearly 40 years of age and still competing against the best riders in the world. All achieved whilst he was working in more than one job and business, and having one passion other than cycling, playing music, my father being a gifted musician.

Apart from Jim's feats in the Tour of Britain, his war hindered capabilities were proven in other races—as well as in other areas of life—too numerous to mention in one book. For example, in one race, after the war, even though Jim was war wounded and past his best years, World Road Race Champion Rik Van Steenbergen could not shake Jim off his wheel, even though Rik tried to kick Jim off his bike!

It is not wheel-sucking, its survival; if one man is stronger than you, you have to level the playing field. Jim would have expected Rik—or anyone in the same boat—if the roles were reversed, to have done the same thing; especially if they had had part of their bowel removed. And depending on form, team tactics and the race situation, even if they hadn't!

As Jim's friend Nev Taylor used to say, when he was threatened after the races for playing dogo and then winning the sprint, *"It's all in the game!"*

"It's all in the game!"

Years later, Mohammad Ali would call a similar tactic in boxing, "Rope a Dope," where Ali would let or make a stronger and younger opponent tire themselves out, whilst he 'rested' on the ropes.

Jim bet Ron Coe that he could not drop him off his wheel, on flat and undulating roads; and even though Ron was younger and a multi-national road race champion, and one of the fastest road sprinters in the world at that time, Ron could not do it.

Which reminds me, Jim said that "Every time Ron met Andre Darrigade in a sprint." Andre was another World Road Race Champion. *"Darrigade finished Second!"* So when it came to bike racing, you didn't want to make an enemy of Jim Wilson, and the same can be said for the author of this book.

Ron Çoe 5 times National Road Race Champion and prolific sprint winner for J.F. Wilson Cycles and Elswick Hopper, both teams were managed by Father

Ron Coe pictured winning the 1958 Bournemouth 3 day stage race, for Elswick Hoppper. Ron's team manager Jim Wilson is pictured 2nd from the reader's right. Jim said "Every time World Road Race Champion, André Darrigade met Ron Coe in a sprint finish, Darrigade finished second"

Lemonade and Turnips

Being left is never a nice thing.

Being left at Dunkirk during World War II, is a totally different thing altogether. Assigned to blow bridges up to stop the German advance, or if not halt it, slow it right down, Jim's unit never made it back in time, from being in front of the front line.

Years later, Jim would say to me that, "Hollywood makes blowing bridges up, look like child's play."

When the reality of rigging bridges, he said was, "Standing up to your neck in bloody cold water for seven hours."

Usually in the dark! Along with being cold, hungry and living in fear of being shot, or if you are not careful, blown up!

Now try and have a sleep for an hour, there in the mud, soaking wet through, no change of uniform here Mr Hanks! Under sporadic attack for days, possibly weeks, depending on your whereabouts and orders.

Where's the nearest public convenience? That bush a luxury! Toilet paper, your trousers.

Your friends have been shot! There's a cow in a tree that has been blown there, but not by the wind. Dead horses in the street with human corpses at your feet, and now the majority of the British army that you belong to have returned back to blighty in retreat.

Chuffing Hell! An understatement. Only one thing to do, move and hide. Preferably Westwards, along the Dunkirk coastline for the time being, in hope of a boat home. Away from the Jerry? Who knows? If the army has pulled out it is anyone's guess. Instinct and wits are crucial now, and the countryside is always the safest place to hide.

And a lemonade factory, hidden in a forest, was an unexpected discovery for Jim and his fellow adventurers; but with the advantage of having something clean to drink. And an unlikely place, even for the SS to seek and destroy.

The only edible food in this neck of the woods, however, was to be found in an outlaying turnip field! Too bad (?) that supermarkets being stamped all over the country was to be over fifty years off into the future.

*

As mentioned, the rigging of certain bridges would take place under the cover of night. Working in the cold black water as the corpses of people and animals floated past you. With no change of dry clothes to change into, to save you private Ryan. No towel, no toilet paper, no so called *super* markets. And you could be shot with real bullets at any time. Surely that would be against health and safety today, and the war would be stopped! In fact both sides were awarded medals for killing as many of the enemy as possible.

After the demolition of the targeted bridges their mission was then to head back to the beaches of Dunkirk and find a boat home.

Which recalls to mind, a story that Doug Petty emailed to me, after we had been reminiscing about my father over the telephone. A story that Jim had told him, years ago in the 1950s, when Jim was Doug's team manager, with the Wilson Cycles racing team: i.e., A View from a Hill, please turn to page 24.

A View from a Hill

Jim's unit arrived at a French village, with orders to 'defend' its bridge from the German advance towards Dunkirk. And having already rigged and primed the bridge with explosives, they climbed to the top of a hill, with a Hawthorn hedge running across its summit, overlooking the bridge and the river.

Directly behind this hedge, they dug a trench, digging it parallel to its base, so that they could lay protected and completely out of sight. Armed with a machine gun and rifles, they could then fire through the bottom of the shrubbery's trunks and stems. They did not have long to wait, before a massive German tank, with a great big gun, came rumbling along the road, heading towards the bridge.

When the tank was in range, they all fired, and Jim said the bullets bounced off the tank, as if they were peas from a peashooter. But this slowed the tank down, to a stop—as the Germans inside the tank could not tell where the firing was coming from. Eventually, the turret with the huge gun, slowly but surely started to swivel round and point up towards the hawthorn bushes at the top of the hill. The other men ran off and left Jim behind.

A big BOOM came from the tank's big gun.

Quickly followed by a bigger BOOM, from the bridge, as it blew a part.

The French family in the farmhouse, at the other side of the bridge from the tank, had boarded up their windows as directed, in readiness for when the bridge was to be blown up. Everyone was in retreat from the German advance. The Jerry were everywhere.

The men had retreated, under the cover of the hawthorn hedgerow, through the farm gate and back to the army lorry. They set off in the lorry without Jim, but he burst through the thick Hawthorn hedge, just in time to run after the lorry at the top of his speed; and after hanging on to the rear of it, by the skin of his fingers, he managed to climb up into the back. It is a pity I cannot print here what my father said, (if anything) after climbing aboard, because knowing Jim, it would have been worth reading.

*

When Jim and his comrades finally arrived on the beaches of Dunkirk, they were too late. All the boats had sailed back across the Channel to England. And the sea and beaches were empty. So they made their way westward, following the coast for a time, travelling by night, avoiding the flashes of warfare, and after camouflaging themselves in foliage, sleeping in ditches and hedgerows in the daytime. As previously mentioned, at some stage of their journey came a spell of hiding in a forest for a while, or should I say hiding in a lemonade factory that they had discovered, hidden in the woods.

Chocolate Canary

At some point, they had to make a move in the open and in daylight. And on one such day, as Jim was walking along and eating some of his plain (dark) chocolate ration, they came under enemy air fire, and he said that the chocolate went hard again in his mouth! He began to run. Being strafed some more, he threw himself face down to the ground, and another soldier, running behind him, ran across his back, stamping his booted foot into the middle of Jim's spine. Jim thought that he had been mortally wounded. Then to his relief, he realised that he was still able to move and quickly found cover.

This along with being quietly patient paid off. Because after travelling on foot for over 420 miles from the beaches of Dunkirk, what was left of Jim's squad, eventually came across a Canadian commando unit, blowing up German fuel dumps, somewhere in the area of St Nazaire. They asked the Canadian soldiers if they could join them on their boat and of course they agreed. And so, like a Roald Dahl twist, when Jim and his army mates finally boarded a boat to escape, it was not from Dunkirk, but from the port of St Nazaire, and the boat did not sail for England. The boat sailed, (for an unknown reason, lost in the history of time), first of all to Spain! Before eventually setting sail for England, at some later date towards the end of the year.

*

Meanwhile, back at home, in his hometown of Sheffield, Jim's mother, Elizabeth, my Grandma Wilson, used to walk down to the local church each day, to look on the blackboard, to see if Jim's name was there, and to find out if there was any news of her son having returned safely back to England…or otherwise.

There was no news. And after some months, there was a funeral for Jim and his fellow comrades in Sheffield town centre. Some confirmed as killed in action, others like Jim, missing in action, presumed dead…their bodies having been washed away in some river, blown to pieces or both.

Eventually, six months later, coming back from Dunkirk (via St Nazire and Spain) to England, and being as it were, on leave, Jim arrived back home in Sheffield (I dare say much to his mother's surprise) just in time for the Sheffield blitz! December 12th to the 15th, 1940.

UXB

When an unexploded bomb was discovered during the war, it was found that it disrupted ongoing, normal life, almost as much as if it had gone off on impact. It became necessary to evacuate whole streets and neighbourhoods, into church halls and community centres, until the danger had been removed.

The people who were detailed to remove the danger, were the British Army Bomb Disposal units. They were supposed to be experts in defusing these bombs and rendering them safe. But the German boffins kept on changing the designs of their weapons, and most of these 'experts' had not a clue what to expect each time they encountered a new type of bomb…Jim was a part of one of these units in England, for a few months, before he was dispatched across the channel again, to fight the 'Hun' on his home ground, or, on what Jerry intended to be his home ground; or in other words, Europe and then the rest of the world.

When a new unexploded bomb was discovered, the unit drove out to the scene in an army truck—the type that is shown in a lot of old films—the ones with a canvas tent, over a steel frame, mounted on the back.

The UXB team usually consisted of six men. Two sat in the front cabin and the other four rode in the back. When they arrived at the site of the UXB, they had to determine if it was ok to explode the bomb where it was, or, if it was in a built-up area, with lots of property around, (like the bomb that went through the roof of Buckingham Palace and failed to explode) then it had to be rendered safe and removed.

I have always thought that this was done in a most professional way…but having listened to this story, passed on from a friend who knew Jim well, I have since had my doubts.

As mentioned earlier, Jim enlisted for a course on bomb disposal, and after a short introductory period, he was therefore on the army's list to be drafted into a small UXB squad when required. And when a UXB was reported, the squad was expected to go out to the danger zone and render the bomb safe, by diffusing or exploding it. This unit in reality consisted of six daring young men of little experience, due to the fact that most of the experts had been blown to pieces learning their trade.

(How to deal with a 1000 LB Unexploded Bomb, Jim style; this extract, is probably related to the story of the bomb that he helped to diffuse in his hometown, at some point after the Sheffield blitz.)

First, locate the device (Usually buried around 15 feet into the ground). Next, build a wall of sandbags about 50 yards or more away from the bomb. Then toss a coin to find out who will be the first two volunteers to start digging out the shell. The lucky winners, set off out, with picks and spades, to proceed the operation, and the rest of the squad hide themselves behind the sandbagged wall.

While the bomb is being dug out, the first two workmen are instructed to create a pit around it, to give enough space for access to the part of the bomb that lets you get to the working bits (usually the clock work part, that is, if it is of that type of bomb!). The two lucky lads carry on digging. The other young fellows behind the wall of sandbags, being sensitive types, decide to encourage the diggers, by calling, or shouting out

"TICKTOCK…TICKTOCK…TICKTOCK."

After 20 minutes of digging, and listening to this encouragement, the diggers retire behind the sandbags, and the next two volunteers go forth to dig; to the accompaniment of *"TICKTOCK…TICKTOCK…TICKTOCK…"* and so forth, until the bomb is exposed, diffused, and safely removed from society.

*

Jim, a sapper in the Royal Engineers, was soon sent back over to occupied France, and for the next five years, fought alongside the allied forces, to push the Germans back.

Impact

Having parachuted down, to land within the perimeter of a barren field, somewhere in German occupied France, my father was now quickly gathering up his parachute.

When, just after the completion of these manoeuvres he heard a fast, increasing whistle coming from above, emanating directly overhead. Jim instinctively looked up, to see something resembling a black ragged dot that was becoming larger every second!

Jim's stance, as he relives this story, suddenly takes on the appearance of a juggler in some kind of bizarre life or death circus act, whose highly thrown and dangerous object has now moved disturbingly out of position.

Instantly, Jim's upper body has now become a cross between, a performer miming a man looking upwards, and at the same time leaning backwards, as if about to limbo under a bar, coupled to an attitude of a teased cobra snake, with the addition of asymmetrical arms and hands, of the wind-blown tight ropewalker. But with legs spread apart, and his feet shuffling quickly, moving the whole weight of his body from one foot to the other, like a boxer on red-hot coals; quickly springing himself from side to side, now looking like the defences, inherent in the fastest crab, only a crab the size of a man. And every sinew filled with, if it was possible at this stage, even more adrenalin. Jim's eyes popping lidlessly outwards, neck craning the head back, from a backbone backwardly sprung; still very focused, looking upwards, trying to work out in which direction to move. Not to catch this object though, but to get out of the way very quickly, away from the incoming plunge of a plummeting and death bound poor soul *whose parachute had not opened!*

By sheer luck for Jim and a lot of calculated agility on his part, the body missed by a matter of yards.

Thud!

The now-corpse, God bless him, had ploughed into Jim's field, and was immediately cast into a mould of firmed down turf and earth, planting itself somewhere in the not so occupied depths of one of France's plentiful terra firma regions.

I say now corpse, because a few seconds before my father had seen a bloke speedily flailing downwards, unswervingly through the sky, at a horrific rate of descent. And now in my father's mind, and possibly at this point, in his imagination, Jim told of seeing the fellow's expression, as if in that instant, deathly moment, he had actually looked into the falling man's eyes for a fleeting nanosecond.

These nightmarish, headlong glances, along with this unfortunate chap's split-second body language of trying to protect himself, with his arms and hands, from the fast approaching Earth, must have been a mind spinning experience, if not a mind blowing sight to witness, even for a soldier! Something that is impossible for any sane human being, ever to become accustomed to, train for, or forget!

After cautiously running over to find the fallen fellow—who, my father soon came to realise, was encased a foot deep into the field, lain face down, with his legs and arms spread akimbo—Jim's duties now were to dig out, retrieve and collect this dead man's dog tag, from the inside of his chest, for identification purposes. And I will always remember Jim saying that, on doing this gruesome task, he had also noticed that the deceased's wristwatch, had embedded itself neatly into this poor Canadian soldier's wrist, such was the impact! The fallen soldier's surname was Pearce. And his Christian name was possibly Clarence—Clarence Pearce.

Doing His Best

During the Second World War, Jim and everyone else concerned, did their best to stop the German advance on Dunkirk; and here are but a few short episodes:

Dressed in workmen's clothing Jim and his fellow soldiers were working on the road, digging it up, to plant explosives in the culverts, near to a bridge. When a big, high ranking German officer's Nazi's car drove up the road with a Swastika on every door.

"Jim, what'll we do?"

Jim saluted the car and hailed them in very good German, good enough for them to return the salute and drive on by.

Jim could speak German fluently. Another time, late in the night, he saw flashing lights from somewhere, deep inside a huge forest, across from the wood that they themselves were occupying. Going over and through the forest's woodland on investigation, he dropped down a hole into a group of German soldiers, firing mortar bombs, at what they thought to be the enemy positions. Jim stayed with them a while, and then said, in confident and confidential German, that he had to go back on duty. On returning to his senior officer to make his report, of German soldiers being in the wood opposite, the captain replied,

"Don't be bloody silly, Wilson."

Boot Loot

Looting was a court martial offence; you could be shot on the spot!

Jim said that there was more fighting during and after the war between themselves over stealing and stolen loot than between themselves and the Germans!

It was November 1944; the allies had invaded Normandy and were pushing their way into Germany. Jim was *already there!* And having an awful time of it, his dress was by now in a dire state!

To be in fashion during a World War a seasoned trooper had to have the right accessories, and they were always on the lookout for an upgrade! The orders were to search all buildings and keep a watch out for any stray German troopers, who might hole up having been cut off from their units, and also to seek and destroy any of the Germans' handy work in the form of booby traps that they were more than likely to encounter along the way.

Jim's unit had been through a lot of 'hassle' by now and they were looking a bit rough around the edges…for weeks with no proper food, a lack of sleep, unwashed and unshaved, basically in a poor way, especially poorly shod in the footwear department. So as instructed they started a methodical search of the buildings…house after house was searched, until Jim found a residence that had obviously been occupied by a German officer of distinction, because around one of the rooms were several objects that only a high-ranking German officer could possess, especially an assortment of black and dark brown leather jack boots ranging in sizes from about 9 to 12. Size 11! Jim thought, 'Just my size,' so Jim sat back and proceeded to try on the boots. 'They fit great.' He strutted up and down the room a bit to get used to them, looked in the mirror and decided they were for him. He then started looking around for anything else that would be useful for the war…when suddenly the door burst open, and in full view to Jim was a blast from the past…in the form of a British officer! Brand spanking new uniform. Arrived that day by plane, straight from Sandhurst military training college.

"What do you think you are doing?!" he demanded…Jim said nothing…

The officer looked at Jim's new boots and said, "This is a looting offence, and you are in big trouble!" Jim said nothing (he was like that). The officer went on for quite a while about the morals of war and the punishment, threatening imprisonment, court martial, and all that…when suddenly the rest of Jim's squad burst into the room. From what I've heard from Jim, he was the only one in this particular unit with any class; the rest were a bunch of low life, ex-criminals, and out for anything they could get. Totally ignoring the rookie officer, they proceeded to ransack the room, turning it over, smashing ornaments and damaging furniture in their attempts to find and steal anything of worth! Before Jim could ask the stunned officer what size and which colour of boots he preferred, the latter had made a hasty retreat, never to be seen again. Jim got his boots, and the war continued.

Paper Millionaires

Scattered around almost every German town, there were loose Deutsche Reichsmark bank notes, dropped by looters, or lost on the wind, from the bank's safes that had been blown or forced open.

Forward to 1976, I'm ten years old.

"Look Dad, I've nearly 40 pounds saved now in my bank book."

He would hold out his hand, without having to say, "Pass it here!" Then picking up a pen from the shop counter, he affected writing into my bankbook. "There, I've added five more noughts on," returning the bankbook back to me. "Now you have, nearly four million pounds!" Casually emphasising, without saying anything, "They're only numbers, just figures in a book."

This was one of those profound demonstrations of his, to provoke thoughts about values in life. A paradox, but with a warmth of humanity that disarmed doubt, even to a kid with questions of clout, it slid into the heart and psyche with such a happy message: Be happy with what you've got, no matter how much or how little, no matter what!

Back to Germany, May 1945, the end of World War II. You could have all the money in Germany now, no one would object because it was worthless. Even if there had been anything left worth buying, you still could not have paid for it with this money. It was now a non-currency. And after all, it was just what it is, paper! Germany had truly lost the war; even its paper was now powerless paper, unless burnt, or written, or drawn upon by a genius.

If you were willing to wait around half a century, possibly die in the meantime, and then, having passed it on, to say your son or daughter, a collector would probably pay a few pounds for a postage stamp or a bank note with Hitler's head on it today—which Jim did not do. I just happened to find these items in an old, carved wooden casket, one day, playing and exploring around the house, as kids used to do; before they became an extension of a computer programmer's computerised future.

These paper treasures were in my parent's attic bedroom, high above our bike shop; and what a magical room—or I should say place—that was; and because of its past associations from that atmospheric time, still is.

I will have to have a good look round our old house again someday, I might find another old memory, that will, no doubt, hold a forgotten story and remind me of some loving and not so loving values. One day. Before they all become sold on *EBay*.

A Wall Away

Huddled together all night under a large tarpaulin cover, away from the wind, cold and chucking down rain, laying on the grass, next to a stonewall, Jim and his army mates perhaps did not have the best of nights' sleep! Standing up to stretch, early the next morning, Jim twisted round and happened to glance over his shoulder—and being tall—also over the wall that was directly behind him. Only to see a dozen German soldiers, doing much the same thing: waking up.

"What did you do? Did you shoot them?" I asked. The answer was a pause, that became silence, and then when I repeated the question, the only reply was:

"What do you *think*?"

Blonde Tuft

"All's fair in love and war."
Winston Churchill

Somewhere, on the soon to be unoccupied side of the Channel, during the war-torn latter stages of the Second World War, there was a bridge. And on this bridge's road this day, lay a blonde-haired, blue-eyed German soldier who had been killed during the fighting.

Germany was now losing the war and there was no need to blow up any more bridges, as the British, with her allies advanced towards Germany. This particular bridge was completely intact, and as all the artilleries, lorries, armoured-cars, jeeps and tanks pounded heavily across its trembling path all day long. Jim said that he noticed that not one of the convoys missed the chance to drive over this unfortunate blonde-haired German! Such was the overall anger at the loss of innocent human life.

By the end of the day, there was hardly anything left of the flattened German, apart from a large tattering rag of grease-stained cloth which was gradually being spread over and into the road's surface. That aside, he was eventually only marked out and identifiable by the survivable relief of a blonde tuft of scalped hair. And because the word had been sent back down the line, that this was the road bridge, with the dead German lying across it, everyone in transit, once arriving at this inhumane crossing, with its pulverised inhuman bridgehead, still aimed for its remaining stain, and happily bumped over the blonde tuft, of hair germane.

Black Bull

Jim along with a newspaper reporter friend are cycling through a bombed and still occupied France, scouting around, when suddenly they came across three surrendering German soldiers. They quickly take away their weapons! It turns out that they belonged to, and are near to, a concentration camp that my father and his paper pal soon discover a little further on down the road.

They tell the Germans to make their way back to their families that are living in the houses of a French village that they have taken over, a few miles further off, saying that they will give them a head start before they open the concentration camp's gates.

As was to be expected, when they do open the gates there is no great surge of revenge from the starved and decimated inmates. My father and his comrades searched for food for them, around the area, and the most substantial edible they could find was a big black bull that was residing in a neighbouring field, which they sacrificed, roasted and shared out to help the remaining survivors to survive.

German Warm Water Torture

Moving through Germany, Jim and his squaddies came across a concentration camp, which had been left and abandoned by the fleeing Germans and those that had surrendered. The stuporous poor souls remaining inside the camp, had no idea that the war was over. My father and his army colleagues broke open the high fenced and barbed doors, to help what was left of those traumatised and emaciated people to get out.

Of the stories that seeped out of a place like this, there were some concerning the different ways in which the German soldiers tortured their inmates. And one story of a method that has always stuck in my mind that Jim *once* told me about, was the warm water torture.

And this is how it goes: When the powers that be, in a place like this, pick on someone that they suspect of having some sort of useful information—usually just a ruse to try a new torture technique out, to see how effective it was—they would select a prisoner for 'interrogation'. After this interrogation, the selected person would then be told that they are going to be executed the next day! Along with some allusion of how it is to be carried out. Twenty-four hours later, the same death expectant prisoner is treated to a repetition of the previous day's cruel inquisition. Following which the inquisitors would then tell the captive in question that the execution has been postponed until the next day. This remorseless trial of abject misery continues indefinitely, which also includes other seriously disturbing mind games, involving the unfortunate individual's forthcoming expiration. The torturers, judging the efficaciousness of this torture on the inmate, keep the prisoner of war at the edge of his wits' end throughout; until the coolest or most insensitive of people, are on the verge of a nervous breakdown or contemplating suicide.

Then all of a sudden, the fateful day arrives, if the 'victim' is still alive! The sufferer is blindfolded, tied to a solid wooden chair, strapped into it by large leather straps around his ankles, chest and forearms; and then told, what he or she has already been continuously led to believe over the preceding weeks: That they are going to be 'executed' by having their wrists slashed open with a razor blade.

For the poor sod, blindfolded with a bag over his head and strapped down firmly into the chair, his or her heart and brain will now be beating to its maximum, as the allusions match up to the rumours *indeed!* Together with sleepless nights and days of built-up stress and drudgery coupled to this moment, one of two things usually happens to these starving human guinea pigs, at this dreaded breaking point: a stroke paralyses or kills them or a heart attack does much of the same terrible or fatal damage. But if this sordid build-up has not affected you in the intended manner formerly described, then there comes *the jug of warm water!*

At exactly the right psychological moment, one of the attendant German soldiers subsequently grabs one of your hands, twisting and turning it, so that the underside of your wrist is facing upwards, and then pressing his extended thumb down into your bared wrist, he draws his thumbnail, slowly but firmly across the exposed, upturned under joint of soft flesh with his free hand. After which he immediately picks up the secretly waiting jug of warm water and quickly pours. Gushing its warm liquid over your prone wrist and lower arm, swiftly repeating the same procedure to your other wrist. Still blindfolded, you now believe that you are bleeding to death. If you are not scared into being dead, you have gone mad by now, and if you have not done either, God help you!

*

The Second World War, culminated for Jim after 6 years, at the far north of the River Elbe. One of the many jobs of a sapper, was to build bailey bridges, but before they could be built over the Elbe, a foothold had to be gained on the far side, to form a bridgehead.

So, after a strong artillery bombardment, in the small hours of the morning of the 29th of April 1945, a part of the British force crossed the Elbe in storm boats. Whilst Jim and his Royal Engineer comrades, were literally in deep water again, building their Bailey bridges, under enemy fire, from land and occasionally from the air. Olive says that Jim and his colleagues rowed across the Elbe; this I cannot confirm or prove but knowing some of Jim's personal feats and the men's character of that era, I would not have put it past them.

When the war ended, Jim stayed in Germany with the army. And in the mess hall, all that the orchestra would play was classical music. Hitler had demanded that throughout Germany, only classical music could be played, and that was what the musicians had grown accustomed to playing well; and so continued to do so for a while after the war.

Jim made a good friend of a German called Heinz—who had been fighting in the war on the Russian front for Germany—and Jim would visit Heinz's family home and bring with him some food that was still quite scarce.

A young child and her mother—friends of Heinz's family—visiting at the same time as my father, who had been told that a British soldier was coming to visit too, caused laughter for Jim, and some embarrassment for the child's mother and their host, when she innocently started singing "We are marching on England…" After a clip round the ear hole from Mum, she refrained.

As an indication of Jim's personality, on the news that he would be returning to England, Heinz's mum cried.

Heinz was a very good racing cyclist, and with Jim they raced in professional six-day races—a form of indoor cycle racing around a track in a velodrome—and also in some major road races on the continent, such as the Tour of Flanders. In fact it was here in Germany, France and

Belgium that Jim learnt the road racing tactics that would put him years ahead of anyone in British cycle racing at that time. There was a professional class for bike racers on the continent, with all its characters, colour, charisma and knowhow. Whereas in England the highest road racing class was known as the Independents…which nevertheless was a step up from what it was before…where riders were only permitted to wear all black, and would have to race very early in the morning to be out of the way, before anyone saw them!

Here is where Jim brought the continent to British cycling…In every way…for one example…Turning 'a snotty nosed kid off the street with nowt' who one day walked into the shop, into a five-times national road race champion and Tour De France rider…His name was Ron Coe, who, with the help of Jim and his team riders, over the years, won all those National championship races (and many other races) for the Wilson Cycles team.

What a Feat! A terraced house shop on City Road with riders in the Tour de France. Ron Coe pictured above in the 1961 Tour De France with Wilson Cycles stitched across his chest racing on his J.F. Wilson bike.

J.F. Wilson cycle frame transfers.

When the big companies finally bought Ron away from Jim, his friend and mentor, and they flew and carried Ron all around the country to race, he never attained those racing heights again. Most people only see the shinning article, they don't care how the golden crown and jewels were forged and set. They did not ask Jim to manage Ron's new team (a team of chiefs with no Indians). And they did not think, or care to take on any of Ron's Wilson Cycles teammates that Jim had formed especially to work so hard for him, and who knew how to sacrifice themselves at the right time, to help Ron into such prolific race winning situations.

Jim understood things. And besides, it always seemed to me that after six years fighting in World War Two, everything that happened to Jim in life was water off a duck's back. Ron was Jim's best man at his wedding. There were no hard feelings. Jim knew that Ron had his own life to lead, with a wife and kids to support. And Ron, who lived out at Sutton cum Lound, would occasionally visit Jim in his shop over the years, long after his cycle racing days.

Jim Wilson was also the most successful team manager that the Elswick Hopper team ever had. All of which again, could fill another book in itself.

On returning to England, after the war, there was a de mob suit and medals waiting for Jim, which were awarded at the end of the war. For whatever personal reason, Jim did not bother with the medals. He was happy just keeping his army number and dog tag as a souvenir. I was told that the de mob suit was too short in the arms for my father; but very little went to waste with Jim, and luckily it fitted his father.

From right to left: Syd Wilson, Jim Wilson (Elswick-Hopper Manager) Harry Reynolds and Ron Coe

After the war, around the age of 27, Jim nursed himself slowly back into normal life. Somehow living in a terraced house at 220 City Road, (that he managed to buy with the help of some money borrowed money from his mother) and turned into a home, (circa 1946) and established a business there in 1948, repairing radios, TVs and bicycles, out of war wound necessity. There was no incapacity benefits then, for having a bone in your leg, my friend. This part of the autobiography reminds me of the film: *It's a wonderful life,* starring James Stewart. Whom my father happened to look very similar to.

After a couple of years fighting shellshock, in 1950, the surgeon who took half of Jim's bowel away, told his mother that he had a year to live. The scar ran down the middle of Jim's abdomen, from his lowest rib to his groin. The injury was brought on from Jim's services in the 2nd World War, that is, being up to his neck in water for hours, blowing bridges up, drinking dirty water and food (if you could find any in the fields) coupled to the other stresses of warfare, that we cannot imagine, and that these men preferred not to talk about.

A year later in 1951, aged 32, still ill, and now far from his best physical condition, Jim raced in and finished 29th overall in the first ever Tour of Britain. And raced in three more of the British tours in 1952, 53, 54. When the race stages were as long and as hard as the proper Tour de France. An era where you carried your spare tyre round your neck and shoulders each stage, with little other help allowed on the road; and when the riders, after each stage, had to find their own digs, repair their own bikes and wash and dry their clothing for the next day's stage. I remember Jim simply saying that certain cycling stars—winners of my generation—'Wouldn't *Finish* some of the races he rode!' All of which to Jim, after six years fighting in WW2, and working every hour God sent, were, I imagine to him, like very tough cycling adventure holidays; gladiatorial cycle race carnivals that he thrived on. That he loved and enjoyed; and was born for.

Even when, before the start of one long stage, someone sabotaged Jim's bike by cutting off nearly all of his seat post, so that he had to ride the whole stage of one hundred plus miles, with the saddle an inch from the top of the top tube.

This picture sums up why Jim was awarded the poster "He Hath Courage" and inspired the title of this book and many other things besides. You can tell by the body language and expression on these men's faces that Jim has pushed himself to near death. The fellow with the boxer's nose is taking Jim's pulse and Jim looks like he is a survivor from a concentration camp. The photo was taken after a stage in the 1951 Tour of Britain. The year before, in 1950, Jim had to have part of his bowel removed, due to services in the Second World War, and the surgeon told his mother (my Grandma Wilson) that he only had a year to live. In 1951 Jim finished 29th overall in the first ever Tour of Britain.

Even when he fell off his bike with other riders on wet tram lines, towards the end of another long stage, and a rider behind him rode into the back of his unprotected head with his front wheel, and fractured Jim's skull as he lay on the road. Jim carried on to the finish.

Years later, when I was a young lad playing around, I happened to place my hand on to the flattened part, at the back of Jim's head, and it was then that my dad casually related to me its cause.

The Tour of Britain was extremely popular at this time, to such an extent that the crowds at the stage finishes required policemen mounted on horses to keep all the spectators back. And just after finishing a gruelling 100-mile-plus stage, Jim crossed the finish line at some speed, only to be knocked off his bike by the swinging backside of a mounted police horse, rearing around and hitting him full in the side of the face. When Jim awoke back to consciousness, he said that hitting that horse's backside, felt just like being hit by a solid sack of cement…and of course he continued to race the next day…

One of Jim's Yorkshire teammates, during the first ever Tour of Britain in 1951, was 20-year-old Doug Petty, and he recalled that, "On one stage, Jim broke away from the start, and was away all day on his own, and it poured down with rain all day. The weather was terrible over Carter bar, and at one point Jim was on the verge of collapse and had to be covered with engine oil to finish the stage."

This could have been the same stage where Jim, having hypothermia, had to be dressed in some of his mother's underwear (Bloomers) to help him to the finish….Otherwise this extra clothing episode would have been in one of the other long and tough races of this era; like The Butlins Tour, (of which Jim won a stage) that started from one Butlins holiday camp on the East coast of Britain and finished at another one of their holidays camp on the West coast; in an era where you never gave up. You either passed out and fell off your bike unconscious or died. Men of Real Proper Steel, who Tommy Simpson, as a young lad would look up to and admire.

Jim Wilson winning a Stage in the Butlins Tour in a Sheffield Phoenix jersey. The crowds at the finishes of stage races in this era were always massive and so was the following. The car was not king. Jim said that some of the factories had bikes packed around them 10 – 20 bikes deep.

Jim was a great bike handler, but he was a phenomenal descender, a very cool man in dangerous situations. Keith Marvin (Jim's team mechanic) recalls, "In one race, Jim was away with a group of riders, and they were flying down a long climb in the rain, when they came to a bend with diesel spread across the camber of the road from a broken down lorry, just before going over a small road bridge, and they all went down like nine pins except for Jim."

Jim modestly said that it was because he was relaxed and did not touch the brakes. Keith said that "When descending with Jim in training, trying to hold on to his rear wheel, you knew you were going fast when the telegraph poles, trees and everything else on each side of you became one big blur."

Jim was one of the world's best descenders that the general public (okay, the world) never knew. He was in a race, riding up a long climb, (somewhere in Wales) in the leading breakaway group, and being about the same height as Merckx, Jim used his head like the great man too, and let the group of climbers he was with go and have their lead, knowing there was a long descent to the finish line, and a better chance of catching them back up on his preferred ground, rather than blowing up on the climb and losing even more ground.

Jim again in a Sheffield Phoenix jersey and you can make out his diamond J.F. logo on the frames' headtube. A frame and bike that he would have hand built himself. Jim was truly part of what they now call the "Golden Generation".

So having gone over the summit of the climb, Jim is now on the decent, traveling at high speed, chasing down the leaders; when all of a sudden, a sheep runs out in front of his path! Going against his natural instinct, he hit the anchors and Jim said, "Both my brake cables snapped up out the of the brake lever hoods." It was as if he had used wire cutters at the nipple heads. (At this time, the brake cables were not hidden under the handlebar tape but came out of the top of the brake levers.) Even so, Jim managed to avoid colliding with the animal and kept on going down the hill with no brakes, with the snapped brake cables dangling in front of him. He caught and passed each one of the breakaway riders as if they were stood still and won the race. One of the riders in the leading break after the race, said that Jim went past him so fast, that he feared for his life; and that it made him want to slow down and pull over to the side of the road; suffering with a sensation akin to vertigo all the way to the finish line.

Think of that; no helmets, tubular tires that you glued on to your wheel rims, and prone to puncture (that would be re used if repairable), that is, if they did not blow out and become unusable. Brake callipers that were so long that when you put them on you went faster! No mobile phones, no air ambulance.

And think of today's riders with disc brakes (on road bikes!), shell helmets, wired on clincher tyres. Can they do 60mph down Winnats pass on their characterless, car-bonfire bicycles? Sure they can; and I'm sure they can travel at 60mph inside their characterless cars as well; with their seatbelts on.

(And today, yes, we all should wear helmets and seat belts, but not necessarily both together.)

In his younger days, Jim had a Norton 900 motorbike that he used to race around on with four other motorbike mad mates; none of them wore helmets. Out of the five of them, three were killed within a year. No wonder my father use to emphasise to me, when I was a young lad, *"If you want to go faster than a bicycle, buy a car!"* And my Grandma Wilson (Jim's mum) used to say to me, *"If you buy a motorbike, I'll come back and haunt you!"*

If you have been used to doing 120mph on a motorbike, what is it to go down a decent at 60mph on a push bike?...To Jim, perhaps, not that fast...Non cyclists reading this, may think that this 60mph statement on a bicycle is an exaggeration...Well, I have been down the Holme Moss descent on my bike—the side of Holme Moss that goes down to Torside, heading on towards Glossop—trying not to use the brakes, and if you had any worries in your life at the summit, (where Jim won the hill prime in the Tour of Britain) they were all forgotten about well before you hit the bottom.

I took a friend for a bike ride in Derbyshire, we rode up Bradwell hill, and took a right at the top, on to the little lane to Windmill, heading for Castleton, via the descent that overlooks the cement works and its charming chimney; and from the highest point in that area, the narrow, snaking road heads down, to go by the side of Pindale. If you know the decent, you will know what my friend meant, when he said that flying down there at some lick, especially around that hairpin bend that brings you round to face in the direction of Winnats pass and that overlooks on your right the appropriately named valley of Hope, that it made him feel like he was on top of a fair ground's Big Dipper ride, sat on the outside of a runaway car that had come off its rails.

One day when Jim spotted me changing my brake blocks, he said, "What are you using your brakes for? You should hardly be touching your brakes in bike races."

Jim, apart from a winter bike (also known to us then as a hack bike, that I would purposely and gladly put together with old, heavy, almost worn out second-hand equipment, from the cellar, that Jim had collected over many years in the shop; yes, it would be a bad advert for a posers shop, but we were the antitheses of a posers shop, and I'm proud to say that at heart we still are today), I only had one race bike to race and train on…and with traffic, and Sheffield and its surrounding areas being hilly, and me a big lad…surely changing my brake blocks once every blue Moon was justifiable….Jim knew it was, but he wanted to instil the idea in to me of not wasting any unnecessary energy (a good habit, especially for successful bike racing; disc breakers) not to mention wasting time and money.

Requiring just the one very good bike to ride (but nothing too fancy to look at.) Jim was the unknowing epitome of Kipling's poem *If—or walk with kings, nor lose the common touch;* I remember that at one point later on in time, that the aluminium of Jim's Campag chain set crank arms were eroded to such an extent, with weathering, wear, and tear that they looked like the texture of those chocolate flake bars that they stick into the top of number 99 ice creams…not the best of adverts to the uninitiated; a subtle statement, similar to a picture in the media that I remember, of Michael Caine, as he purposely crouches down by the side of a big dint in the front wing of his Rolls Royce. But Jim, luckily, was not a millionaire in monetary terms, nor famous, and it had nothing to do with bragging rights.

In his younger, racing days, when chainsets were made of steel, like the character of his generation, Jim would put house bricks in his saddle bag, to make his bike heavier in the winter season; to feel the benefit at the start of the racing season, when he would take the saddle bag off, and his winter, club run, touring bike became his racing bike again.

Jim came from a hard time—necessity wise—appreciative generation and would sometimes only put the shop lights on when a customer came into the shop; and the *sometimes* means not necessarily even then.

And if it was cold, you wore extra clothing and drilled through a few blank front fork crowns, using an old hand operated wheel drill on a stand, in the shop's cellar, to create a front brake calliper bolt hole, or sawed through some wood. Wood that would finally come in handy for a big old boiler that Jim had found somewhere and took four men to move and carry down into the shop cellar.

Once upon on time there was no such thing as central heating. And no horrible energy companies taking lots of money off you for the set ups they put in your house that you do not really need.

It's not in their interests for their so called 'smart' metres to work, so they very often don't; it is in their interest for them to be what they are, dumb meters, and not to work and overestimate your bill. And take even more money off you. Notice that they never underestimate your bill. Even if you used no energy there is a corrupt standing charge for having one of their meters.

Only two bikes! So what? Jim, (As did most of his generation, only had the one bike for all the year, and possibly a career. So when someone like Jim said, "What are you using your brakes for? You should hardly be touching your brakes." You listened.

In the Tour of Britain, there was a stage where Jim was flying down a steep, twisting descent, and to avoid a car coming the other way on a tight bend, he had no other option than to hit a dry stone wall, that he was catapulted over, bike and all, into a muddy field, landing on his chest and face first, and on coming round Jim was laid out in the mud on his back by some people he recognised, but who did not recognise him, and Jim said that he thought to himself, *'Oh dear! I must be in a very bad way.'*

There was once a road race that had a 100-mile neutralised start to it, before the race started properly, to race another 150 miles, totalling 250 miles! Jim said that when they dropped the flag after the 100-mile neutralised section to start the race, all the riders stopped, sat down at the side of the road, and devoured their food in protest. Then they got on their bikes and raced 150 miles. I hope the drug cheating professionals that moan that the Tour de France is too long read this. Because if they put a couple of 200-mile stages in the Tour it would get rid of you from the sport and any other snowflake stars. Because your drugs would be no good, even if your small mindedness could cope with facing the monotony of a real grand bike race, the amount you'd need would be a detriment to you or kill you, so it would be down to guts and heart. And a true love for riding your bike.

I doubted Jim's 'they wouldn't *finish* some of the races he rode' remark, about the winners of my generation, at first, as an indifferent youth, and a little further on, as a carefree, confident young man. But over many years, a slow dawning has come to me of his meaning. I now realise that if those riders had been through the same as you Jim, and been inwardly disabled as you were, that that would be only too true. Because they would not have had it in them to start the race in the first place. And if they had started this sort of Tour of Britain, in the same physical and psychological condition that you were in, lacking your Dunkirk spirit, and in that kind of hard era, I really do believe, that they would not have finished a stage, let alone the full Tour. In hindsight, all things considered Jim, you were right, and still are. More so, as things have only become softer and lightweight the more the years pass by. Or in other words, not as good. Like bike, like rider and vice versa.

Jim taught, not by long-winded explanations, but by little gems of knowledge, (to the extent that you did not feel like you were being taught at the time) letting you figure things out for yourself. And he would only give you good advice once; very rarely did he repeat it. Unless he had forgotten that he had already said it, and that could be years later.

And even then, would you listen? A young man only sees an old man; and one that is not world famous or rich. I did not realise it at the time, but Jim was like a modern-day Socrates, only he did not have to talk as much, and so avoided a lot of trouble that saved time for much more positive projects. In my opinion that is a wiser course. Jim could have taught Epictetus and Marcus Aurelius on 'what is the right way to live'. And like those great philosophers, Epictetus and Socrates, Jim did not write anything down. Others inspired by their actions in life, did that for them.

Nevertheless, Jim's wisdom would eventually get through to me. The above kind of knowledge once gained, never leaves you, and so becomes a type of wisdom in itself.

Jim was an exceptional teacher. He must have been, to have some effect on a stubborn, block head like me; Jim really did have the patience of a saint. His wealth—you just knew—was in his knowledge. And Jim's knowledge was that of wisdom. He or she who is wise, will be wealthy and famous enough for the whole of their life.

Jim seemed to only *talk* when things mattered. Otherwise his dialogue was quiet but engaging.... Every now and then, Jim would remind me of the saying,

"See all, hear all and say nowt."

Before social media, when people actually had the balls to talk to each other, some other sayings doing the rounds at that time were:

"Laugh and the whole world laughs along with you, cry and you cry alone."

"If you can't say owt good, don't say it."

I remember as a young lad, standing at the side of my father, watching him play his beloved Hammond organ in our living room at the back of the shop; sometimes he would try to teach me a few little things on the keyboard. Letting me run up and down all the keys (black and white) in a well know fingering practice.

Once I asked, "Why are there these particular notes in the chord of C?" And he replied, "Because they are." And I would continue, "Why isn't there a chord of K or Z? And Jim would close his eyes and play some lovely melody in reply. Possibly hoping that I had drifted away, to fool about somewhere else when he reopened them. But with Jim, it always seemed that he did not mind either way. And that made you wonder to yourself whether asking questions like these were not your loss. But I do not think they were…because if Jim had known the answers or thought them important to living, he would have happily tried to explain them. In other words, if you are that bothered about such questions, find out for yourself in your own time, not while I'm enjoying playing the organ."

Jim Wilson playing the blues on his Hammond organ on German TV…backing Champion Jack Dupree

By the way, after the war, Jim was ill and in regular daily pain and discomfort for the rest of his life. But you would not have known it, or at least to have known to what extent. Because apart from when nature called, he did not show many signs, and he certainly did not talk about it. Occasionally holding on to a wall, whilst he tried to get to the toilet was about the only obvious sign. And yet I would say that he was as happy as any man could be in life. And years later, when he would leave the shop for the last time, to go into Western Park hospital, for a much too late cancer chemo treatment, he politely held my helping arm of assistance away, to walk out by himself to the waiting ambulance.

The last time I saw my father, he was in a bed at Western Park Hospital, and it was sad to see Jim spaced out on cancer treatment drugs. It was not nice for me to see him rambling to himself, some unpleasant things from his past…I must have known it was going to be this way, an inspired intuition, or simply a guess? As this was the only time, before visiting, that I looked for, found and brought along my Walkman (that I rarely used) with a cassette tape fitted into it of Jack Dupree playing and singing the blues. I placed the headphones into Jim's ears and a smile lit up his face, and typically, with his eyelids drawn down and his head gently swaying to the rhythm of the music that he had sung, played and loved for most of his life, his hands started to play his much-loved Hammond organ over the bed sheets.

I left the room without disturbing Jim, other than a wave of goodbye and perhaps a hug and a kiss, I cannot quite remember…but I know this – that at that moment with or without those gestures of love – we were both satisfied.

His undiagnosed prostate cancer pain in Jim's last years, was initially, probably mistaken as part of the bowl operation, war wound pain that he had quietly lived with for forty-four years.

I remember, one day I was working behind the counter in the shop, when Jim's doctor came into the shop, (could you imagine that happening today?) and asked if my father was in, I said no he was next door.

Jim on his way to France with The Four Blades. Note the bikes on top of his car and his Hammond organ in tow, epitomize Jim's love of life.

The doctor said, "Don't tell your dad, but he has cancer…." At some point, Dr M had driven past Jim going up City Road from his D---- Street Medical practise and had seen Jim leaning on a wall, with his other hand holding his back; to this day, I'm not sure if the doctor had had any other evidence, or whether Dr M just knew the sign from experience. At that time we had just about bought the house next door to the shop, after living in it with lodgers and students to help pay the mortgage; it took 20 years! (The exclamation mark is because the value of the house was the same price as an average priced, overpriced, almost worthless plastic bike costs today, that is paid for on the spot with a small plastic card) …so here it is again, it took 20 years! With students and other lodgers living with us for a good number of those years. Such are the banks' life crippling interest charges.

In my view, Mr Hitler's war and its knock-on effects had prematurely killed another person. Jim's mother and brother had both lived into their nineties. Jim was 74.

I never heard my father swear, and I have just reminded myself, whilst writing the above, that throughout our life together, I never heard him moan about anything of a personal nature.

Even with the help of the bike shop and hairdressing businesses' income; where Jim for decades, charged 50p for a wheel truing and Olive charged the same price for a haircut. And everything else was under charged; but here is where the old adage, *you get what you pay for,* went out of the window with a strong tailwind, because we built and trued very good wheels and bikes, and Olive was a very good hairdresser. When my mum washed your hair, it was like having a proper Indian head massage; in other words, she massaged your scalp to stimulate healthy hair growth, but with the addition of warm water, shampoo and conditioner. Afterwards, not only your hair and scalp, but you yourself felt invigorated. And we built wheels, frames and bikes for some of the best riders in the country, at a price most people could afford…and if my mother or father heard or thought that you could not afford it, they would help you out. No wonder they were both loved and respected by their customers and the community that they lived in.

So for convenience, and mine and my mum's sanity, we had eventually bought the house next door—not for Jim's sanity because he could have lived and worked almost anywhere, because he was living doing what he loved; it was only because of a semi-humorous hint at a divorce, and the luck of the house next door coming up for sale at the same time, that made for a happy change for us all—and we were able to knock through from 220 City road to 222 City road, and at the same time doubling the garden space and procuring a good-sized, outside workshop: we no longer had to build and braze our frames in the shop's cellar.

The cellar reminds me of taking those large, heavy, five foot tall, oxygen bottles down the shop's sloping side passage, from the waiting lorry—or sometimes the bottle was just left by the driver, laid flat on the floor in front of the shop window—through three gates, in to the yard, and then taking out the cellar window (that was at that time only held in by two old nails) before lowering them into the cellar. It was a bit of feat in itself looking back. Jim had been doing this for years, before I was born and long before I was strong enough to help.

You could not physically lift up one of those solid steel bottles, each one had to be twirled along the ground at a slight angle, almost upright, it was a knack you had to master, or else; if a bottle went over at the wrong angle, it would pull you over with it, like a black belt in judo.

I used to visit the same dentist as my father, and when one day the dentist asked me if I would like an anaesthetic painkiller for a filling, I said, "Yes please!" And possibly because of my slight intonation of surprise, he mentioned that "Your father does not have one," and that, "Mr Wilson usually falls asleep whilst I work on fillings and removals." Mr K, our dentist, was an Indian gentleman, with a turban, gold-rimmed glasses, a Rolls Royce and a full-face black beard, and very rarely spoke about anything, other than the necessary procedures of dentistry, and even then, sparsely. In other words he was a seriously professional man, and in no way inclined to chitchat, let alone exaggerated storytelling. Jim never mentioned this episode to me, until I asked him about it, at some point later, when it came to my mind in conversation. He showed me the metal bar of an implant sticking out of his gum, where an upper, left-hand-side incisor should be. That bar he mentioned, was going to have a tooth screwed on to it later, when the tooth was finished. He said that the drilling into the bone of his jaw was something he would not forget. I can hardly believe that Jim would not have had some anaesthetic for that. But then again, I dare say that the surgeon that gave Jim a year to live in 1950, would hardly believe that he raced in one of cycling's hardest national tours the following year. The same year that the surgeon had predicted that Jim would probably die!

After the 1951 Tour of Britain, the Sheffield Phoenix cycling club, at their club dinner, awarded Jim with a simple paper poster, with a black and white portrait photograph of himself stuck in the middle. It shows Jim wearing over his woollen jersey, a spare tubular tyre, snaking under his armpits, and around his neck and shoulders, a simple white hoppy cap turned backwards, some sunglasses and an enigmatic smile with these simple words, boldly handwritten above it:

Jim Wilson

He Hath Courage

Poster awarded to Jim Wilson by the Sheffield Phoenix Cycling Club after the first ever Tour of Britain in 1951. The inspiration that created the Sheffield Phoenix's Courage Cup.

This tribute meant more to the membership, and to those people who knew of Jim's exploits at that time, than any Oscar. Or for that matter the sports personality of the year awards.

Jim's feats of courage were also the inspiration that created the Sheffield Phoenix's solid silver courage cup. No ordinary trophy was produced either. It stood about twenty inches high, in the form of a tall, athletic, naked man, with a laurel wreath crown resting on his head, and with one arm raised above this crown in a victory wave or salute; the other arm is by his side holding another laurel in his hand. This trophy was created for Jim and awarded to him for his sporting endeavours, even though inwardly disabled by the war. A trophy, which Jim handed straight back to them, to be awarded, not annually! Nor necessarily given for just winning races. But presented for exceptional courage in the face of severe adversity. I heard—whether jokingly or not—that the trophy had to be kept in the town hall safe.

Jim achieved all of the above whilst working full time wherever possible, and in more than one job. He worked on building sites, as well as in the bike shop. And some nights played with various groups on his beloved Hammond organ. All primarily to support the shop, which was also Jim's home. No war pension, no incapacity benefit. Men like Jim would not accept that fate, even if there were any to accept. And in my opinion, it is that instinctive, natural mindset that makes them great. Olive said that once some government official had come to see Jim about some so-called assistance, and she said Jim just happened to vanish around the same time.

One story of Jim working on building sites sticks in my memory, and it was of an incident as a roofer: I had walked into our living room from school, or from playing outside, and Jim is laying back in a chair, in pain, in the living room, at the back of our shop house, with red whirls showing through his bandages that were wrapped around the lower part of his legs up to his knees. My dad had received these injuries, after having walked on a roof that had not been finished off and had been covered over with a tarpaulin. Through the roof Jim fell, into a metal vat of hot pitch that was stationed below…to remove the pitch from his shins later in hospital, it had to be peeled off, along with his skin…Jim said that more than one nurse fainted.

In 1953, Doug Petty signed as an Independent for Wilson Cycles of Sheffield; assigned the job of tea-boy for Belgian racing trips: Jim let Doug know that "*They don't 'ave tea over there kid.*"

Doug suffered his first telling-off when his mum bought tea from Keithley market, "WHAT'S THIS!" bellowed Jim. "Er…it's t-tea Mr Wilson," stuttered Doug.

"We're goin' to tak thi abroad kid," said Jim latter. "Whatever they've telled thi, it's six times better." When they saw a huge field of rugged Belgiums, lined up for a race near Ghent, one of the team blurted out, *"These aren't cyclist, there bloody wrestlers!"*

Doug found himself at the front; and as one or two were struggling, he decided, "I'll just slow the race down a bit for the team."

"A big, hairy hand came out of the bunch and gripped me from behind and shot me backwards, then another hand did the same, and another and another, till I were out the back!"

"I forgot to tell thi kid—they don't do teamwork 'ere!" Jim commented afterwards.

At another race, the rookie as keen as ever: "What's the tactics for today, Jim? *Ang on as long as tha can*!"

Head down in another race, Ken Stratford hit a post and fetched six riders off. Jim collared Doug at the finish, "Kid, if tha sees Ken, tell im not to come back 'ere. They're goin' ter kill him."

The photo shows Syd Wilson to the reader's left, 10 years younger than his brother Jim, and to the reader's right Doug Petty.

Another young youth who visited Jim's shop, was Tommy Simpson. "On a couple of occasions Jim repaired Tom's bike in an emergency, the day before his races (and for nowt) according to Keith Marvin, Jim's Tour of Britain team mechanic and regular helper in the shop.

"One Saturday, Tommy put his gear in his wheel and snapped the frame's rear dropout off, Jim brazed him a new dropout in the same day and set Tommy's bike back up for his race on Sunday."

Keith loved to be around Jim and all the characters that Wilson Cycles attracted, and he'd help out his mentor for his dinner and tea and payment in kind; to Keith it was a privilege…and a dream job!

Years later, Professional World Road Race Champion Tommy Simpson invited Jim and Olive to stay at his hotel restaurant in Belgium.

The book's author being held up by his father, outside Tommy Simpson's hotel restaurant.

Ken Russell, the winner of the 1952 Tour of Britain, when interviewed by Nigel Land for his relatively recent book about the Elswick Hopper team, asked Ken who built his racing frames, and Ken said, "A little shop on City Road in Sheffield."

"I would only let Jim Wilson build my best racing frames."

It was a shame my father was no longer around for Nigel to talk to, as Jim was also the team manager of the successful Elswick Hopper cycle racing team and would no doubt have had some marvellous inside stories to relate about the team and how they achieved their race winning results.

Jim Wilson was made a life member of the *Sheffield Phoenix Cycling Club,* having over many years encouraged hundreds of people new to cycling and cycle racing. A respected figure, having been an independent racing cyclist and founder and rider manager of the Wilson Cycles Team that took riders to race in the Tour De France as part of a National team. Jim himself had numerous placings aboard in Semi-Classics, for example, sixth place in Hanover—Brunswick and rides and *finishes* in Classics such as the Tour of Flanders.

(Singer Sewing Machine Co.)
March 1959.

Fine Feathers . . .

make fine birds, and fine birds, finer.

Our picture shows the famous Elswick-Hopper cycle team wearing their very smart Singer-embroidered jerseys. Last season the team won twenty-three road races, an all-time record.

The team came down from the North of England to be guests of honour at a big reception, given at a famous London hotel, to launch a new type of bicycle made of reinforced plastic. It was suddenly decided that the team should have their jerseys embroidered with their names and other details, and the order was placed with our Embroidery Department.

This was a real 'rush job', and two jerseys for each team member were completed in record time.

The team also wore their jerseys at the Cycle Show at Earls Court, where they aroused great interest. One newspaper commented that the jerseys were the brightest patch of colour in the Show!

1959

Jim Wilson (center back) Elswick Hopper rider and Team Manager with left to right: National Road Race Champion Ron Coe, Army Champion Harry Reynolds, Frank Clements, Alan Bladon and Syd Wilson. With Jim Wilson as manager the team won 23 races in 1958, an all-time record.

Jim was a highly successful team manager, and he also found sponsorships such as Ovaltine, Airlite, Benelux, Tizer (BARR), Saxa salt, Hi-Lift, Dare Grips, O'Brien, Alp, Singer (sewing machines) and I dare say many others…to create and run various winning teams, one of which was the *Elswick Hopper* Team in 1958.

In short, Jim Wilson was an amazing bike rider, athlete and person, considering he had come back from near fatal injuries after being left to fend for himself on the beaches at Dunkirk and German occupied France.

These feats proved to be a Great Inspiration to many other people at that time, and they still do—to those who care to know—today!

My father's greatest talent was bringing people together from all walks of life, and selflessly making them into something greater than they may have realised; being left to themselves and society.

Peter Ward, the author of *Champion of Champions* dedicated a good deal of the wisdom and racing knowledge in his book to my father. Peter is pictured at the back of his book riding for Jim's highly successful Wilson Cycles team.

One year, in 1957, the team achieved an all-time record number of road race firsts, along with winning a prolific five National Road Race Championships over the years with Ron Coe.

And when Dave Orford won the Gold medal at the World Veteran Road Race Championships in Austria, the first thing Dave did was to dedicate his gold medal and Rainbow jersey to his lifelong friend and mentor—Jim Wilson.

When Dave Orford won the World Road Race Championships in Austria, the first thing Dave did was to dedicate his gold medal and Rainbow jersey to his lifelong friend and mentor, Jim Wilson.

The above photograph shows Dave as a young man, 3rd from left, along with from left to right John Bennett, Doug Petty, Ken Stratford, Syd Wilson and rider manager Jim Wilson.

From World Champions, to Tour of Britain winners and Tour de France riders, to top national and international road race and cyclo-cross riders, to local customers and club cyclists:

One of many customers reminisces: "As a kid of about twelve, I was a keen cyclist and still am 60 years later. I used to go to Jim's shop on City Road, as I had a paper round at that time, and used to save up my 10 bob (ten shillings) or 50 pence a week to spend on my bike. I remember one time I was in the shop, and was looking at some really well made, perforated leather, Italian cycling shoes (I had never had proper cycling shoes) and I couldn't in a month of Sundays afford this lovely leather pair. After about two hours hanging about (Jim never used to mind how long you hung around) I told him I was off. Just as I opened the shop door to leave, Jim threw the shoes to me, and I told him I couldn't afford them. Jim just quietly said, "Take 'em. I know you will pay me if you can." It took me a few weeks to pay Jim in bits and bobs at a time, but he never asked for owt. I have never forgotten Jim's generosity and trust, and witnessed it on many occasions, a true gentleman."

Club cyclist and customer, Judd Newton Cutts: "We was out in Derbyshire on a Sunday run, when a bloke on a rusty old Wilson came flying past, and we all said the same thing. *That's Syd Wilson's bike!* So we followed him to a house on Windy Hill Lane, and next day Syd fetched the bike back. It had been pinched from outside his brother's bike shop, and was instantly recognisable, as the frame was unsprayed and red rusty."

(NB. The above story would have been from 1959; and the reason for the unfinished and rusty looking frame, was that a few weeks before the Manx Road Race, Syd crashed and smashed up his frame, and although his brother Jim could replace Syd's damaged frame tubes in time, it was not possible to stove enamel the frame before the Isle of Man Race. And then on top of that, Syd's bike was stolen the week before the Isle of Man Classic Race. Luckily Judd saved the day. And the Wilson Cycles team and the other British teams i.e. Ovaltine Alp, O'Brien Wilson that Jim helped to form and bring to the IOM that year, by all accounts, had a good race and a great time. And as Jim half-jokingly noted, the frame would weigh less without paint…it was said to have been a bit of a head turner, the fancy, hand cut lugs having been, as it were, lined in brass, showed off Jim's craftsmanship at a whole new level.)

Another customer remembers the time when he was a young lad on a club run in Derbyshire, and he had been left behind going over Owlar Bar, and how Jim had waited and looked after him, pushing him up the hill and showing him the way to the café. "And making sure I made it home. To me, it was wonderful to be looked after in this way by my hero."

Doug Petty, raced in the legendary Manx Premier International Road Race on the Isle of Man on the 17th June 1959—also known as the 'Coppi Race'.

There were 25 continental riders in five teams: including three Tour de France winners—besides Coppi. Completing the start sheet, were fifty-three British based Professionals! (aka Independents) The O'brien Wilson

Team were: 39 Dave Bedwell: 40 J.F. Wilson; 41 Syd Wilson; 42 Alan Bladon; 43 Doug Petty; 44 JA George.

Other teams Jim helped to have a place in this race apart from the Wilson Cycles team and Elswick Hopper were the Ovaltine Alp, O'Brien Wilson and Langsett teams.

At the start of the legendary Manx Premier International Road Race – also known as the "Coppi Race" Syd and Jim Wilson can be seen in WILSON CYCLES light blue with black sleeve jerseys and red caps at the back. Left of picture is 5 times Winner of the Tour de France, Jacques Anquetil. On the front row Raphaël Géminiani is standing next to Fausto Coppi. Also, you can spot the race Winner André Darrigade, Raymond Poulidor, Doug Petty and Shay Elliott.

Doug recalls, "Dave Orford said, 'I'll get on Bobet's wheel.' Then he punctured. Coppi did a huge effort and split the field to pieces. Andre Darrigade attacked and went up to the break. I hung on his wheel, and he took me up and then he went on to win the race."

Jim was riding with Fausto Coppi on a climb in the 1959 Manx race, (by this time Jim was nearly 40 years old, and Fausto was only a few months younger than Jim). And Jim said, then I was riding behind Fausto, as Coppi was being pushed up the climb by two of his teammates, one on each side of him.

The race officials looked the other way. After all, this was Fausto Coppi racing on British roads, for the first time in his life (and sadly for the last); and also, perhaps the commissaries turned a blind eye, because Fausto was no longer in contention of winning the race by that point. It must have been a hard racing season for Fausto that year. Unfortunately, Fausto Coppi died of malaria in early January the following year, caught on a hunting trip to Africa with Raphael Geminiani. Raphael also caught malaria on the same trip but managed to survive.

MANX PREMIER

Professional Road Race

WEDNESDAY, 17th JUNE, 1959

10 Laps Clypse Circuit (100 miles) **Start: 10-30 a.m.**

1.	**F. Coppi** (Italy)	Coppi
2.	**A. Kazianka** (Poland)	Coppi
3.	**G. Boni** (Italy)	Coppi
4.	**M. Gismondi** (Italy)	Coppi
5.	**C. Cassano** (Italy)	Coppi
6.	**L. Bobet** (France)	Mercier
7.	**J. Bobet** (France)	Mercier
8.	**P. Gouget** (France)	Mercier
9.	**A. Dupre** (France)	Mercier
10.	**J. Andrews** (England)	Mercier
11.	**J. Anquetil** (France)	Helyett
12.	**A. Darrigade** (France)	Helyett
13.	**J. Plaudet** (France)	Helyett
14.	**E. Delberghe** (France)	Helyett
15.	**S. Elliott** (Ireland)	Helyett
16.	**R. Geminiani** (France)	Geminiani
17.	**P. Everaert** (France)	Geminiani
18.	**B. Robinson** (England)	Geminiani
19.	**M. Dejouhannet** (France)	Geminiani
20.	**P. De Haan** (Holland)	Geminiani
21.	**R. Walkowiak** (France)	Peugeot
22.	**C. Le Menn** (France)	Peugeot
23.	**P. Ruby** (France)	Peugeot
24.	**C. Colette** (France)	Peugeot
25.	**M. Rohrbach** (France)	Peugeot
26.	**A. S. Brittain**	Viking Cycles
27.	**B. Haskell**	Viking Cycles
28.	**G. O'Brien**	Viking Cycles
29.	**T. W. Oldfield**	Viking Cycles
30.	**J. A. Ryan**	Viking Cycles
31.	**R. Coe**	Elswick-Hopper
32.	**O. G. Blower**	Elswick-Hopper
33.	**J. R. Geddes**	Elswick-Hopper
34.	**H. T. Reynolds**	Elswick-Hopper
35.	**F. R. A. Clements**	Elswick-Hopper
36.	**J. de Roo** (Holland)	Middlekamp
37.	**P. L. Rentmeester** (Holland)	Middlekamp
38.	**J. J. Huissoon** (Holland)	Middlekamp
39.	**D. Bedwell**	O'Brien-Wilson
40.	**J. F. Wilson**	O'Brien-Wilson
41.	**S. Wilson**	O'Brien-Wilson
42.	**A. Bladon**	O'Brien-Wilson
43.	**D. Petty**	O'Brien-Wilson
44.	**J. A. George**	O'Brien-Wilson
45.	**J. P. Murphy** (Canada)	—
46.	**B. Clayton**	Langsett
47.	**A. Williamson**	Langsett
48.	**K. A. Lyne**	Langsett
49.	**M. Coupe**	Langsett
50.	**B. C. Pusey**	Witcomb Trading
51.	**D. H. Orford**	Ovaltine-Alp
52.	**A. Hoyland**	Ovaltine-Alp
53.	**P. McFarlane**	Ovaltine-Alp
54.	**P. A. Ryalls**	Ovaltine-Alp
55.	**G. Shaw**	Ovaltine-Alp
56.	**B. Trippett**	Ovaltine-Alp
57.	**M. Horder** (Australia)	Wally Green
58.	**J. Morris**	Wally Green
59.	**F. Ward**	Wally Green
60.	**R. Spencer**	Wally Green
61.	**T. Smith**	Wally Green
62.	**I. F. Brown**	Armstrong
63.	**A. R. Hitchen**	Ellis Briggs
64.	**P. Ellison**	Ellis Briggs
65.	**K. W. Balmforth**	Ellis Briggs
66.	**K. Jowett**	Ellis Briggs
67.	**A. J. Kershaw**	Sid Mottram
68.	**D. Etchells**	Sid Mottram
69.	**E. White**	Sid Mottram
70.	**J. Bennett**	Sid Mottram
71.	**P. Street**	Bev Wood-Silkin
72.	**R. J. Magee**	Bev-Wood-Silkin
73.	**A. Hope**	Bev Wood-Silkin
74.	**P. Nowell**	Lune R.C.C.
75.	**A. B. Keenahan**	Tame Valley
76.	**G. J. Vines**	Condor
77.	**D. Hutton**	Jack Hearne
78.	**R. L. Sunderland**	—

Alan Bladon Wilson Cycles races alongside Fausto Coppi in the legendary 1959 Max Road Race.

Caught Short

Jim was cycling up City Road, wearing a pair of ex-army khaki shorts, riding alongside a row of slow-moving vehicles, held up by a funeral possession, going to City Road Cemetery a little further up the hill.

Then an old car, with forward facing door handles, came up close behind him, and as it passed, the door handle caught in the pocket of Jim's shorts.

Jim told Olive that, "One second I was on my bike…the next second, I was running alongside the car…and the next second, I was standing outside the shop in my underpants."

Incident of Indecent Exposure

Jim was on one of his trips to France with Olive, travelling through Brittany in his Atlas three-geared van. When suddenly, due to his war wound complaint, he had to go to the toilet.

Being in the open countryside, he looked for a bush or a wall, or some sort of private place for cover. Then he spotted a clump of bushes, beside the road. Ideal! He thought. So he jumped out of the van in a hurry, ran behind the bushes, and into a wheat field. (And probably not quite in his own words, this story having been passed on to me), He, 'dropped his shorts, cocked up his arse and started to crap'.

Just as he started, he heard the noise of an approaching vehicle, Jim looked round, and to his horror, he saw a bus pulling up behind him, on a road running parallel to the road he had stopped on, that would join with the main road, about 50 metres further on. The bus's road itself having been obscured by the height of the wheat. But the bus's windows overlooked the wheat. He also saw about fifty female pensioners, looking at 'his arse in action', as the bus passed, slowing down for the junction, which was when Jim noticed the GB plate on the back of the bus…British tourists!

And he consoled his shame, by believing that the passengers would just assume that they had witnessed the actions of a dirty French farmer, working in his fields.

Jim and Olive above and below, loved to holiday in France, sometimes with the group, The Four Blades, and sometimes for the cycle racing, both business and pleasure.

*

My father took an interest in most things, but his other main love was music. As an accomplished organist, Jim played the Hammond organ with his lifelong friend, Jack Dupree, in Jack's band the Premonitions, but also at home. I remember hearing them both playing and singing downstairs at nighttime when I was a young boy in bed above the shop. The Premonitions included a very talented guitar player called Granville Hill. Granville said that he had many a good joke and a laugh with my father and remembers Jim talking about his WW2 days and relating a story or two that I have included in this book, one of war and one of music.

Jim Wilson, with his bike and Jack Dupree with his car. Jack's car door reads "Champion Jack Dupree" Blues Pianist of NEW ORLEANS LA USA

Milk, Rock 'n Roll, Alcohol Abuse and a Strange American Sausage Stew

Jim supported his cycle shop business for a number of years working on building sites as a roofer during parts of the day and in the evenings. Sometimes playing the keyboards with various well-known singers and groups around the region at night. When I was growing up and practicing on the electric bass guitar, Jim used to say to me, "If you ever want to a have play, go and see Frank White, he'll let you join in." I never got round to that but played a gig on bass in Sheffield's Octagon theatre in my teens, with a Rock and Roll band called *The 57s*. We were filmed, along with every other band that went up on stage. I have never seen any footage and was never fussed about it; although 40 years on it would be interesting now, to see myself playing my second-hand, sunburst coloured bass on stage in hipster flares and a sleeveless, woollen, V-neck tank top. I mention this for Jim's laid-back approach to life that was bound to rub off on to me to some degree.

I turned up to this music festival at the Octagon after having gone training on my bike all morning, arriving with bass in hand, just about as we were to go on stage; I did not think anything of it; sometime afterwards, when I met up with my young band mates again, they said they couldn't believe I just turned up and played like it was some practice session, and were amused, taking it well; they could see it was not something I had done intentionally, so fortunately to them it came across as being a pretty cool thing.

After working in the shop, training on the bike came first and was rarely interrupted; for me, music was just something to do now and then during the winter months. Jim's quiet influence on me was profound if not amazing. As a young boy, I loathed going cycling and probably would never have considered playing a musical instrument either. And here I was, racing and training with some of the best professional riders in the country, and performing, or should I say, playing music on stage for fun.

At some point Jim played or guested with famous bands such as Cream, Steel Eye Span and Mott the Hoople. Culminating in appearing playing the organ on German television with Jack Dupree; they were filmed at the famous Beat Club in Bremen, by EDF the national public TV channel.

For me personally, and for Jim too, I'm sure, that was the most musically enjoyable and satisfying time, when my father was backing his good friend Jack Dupree, fondly known to me from being a young boy as 'Uncle Jack'. But in the music world, Jack was universally known as *Champion Jack Dupree*. Jack was a brilliant, original blues singer and pianist from Chicago…And in Jack's younger days he was a Champion boxer, where the title came from and stuck.

When I was about three or four years old, I remember Jim, Olive and myself visiting Jack's family in Halifax. And I recall being in their kitchen and watching the stirrings of a deliciously smelling and bubbling hot stew which amongst many other ingredients, contained full-length, individual, uncut banana-shaped sausages that kept bobbing up to the surface for air, looking to me as a kid, like the humped backs of miniature whales or the flanks of little Nessies.

For later generations, Jack's the same guy that plays the piano and sings on one of Budweiser's TV adverts; do not think I'm mistaking him for TJ Hooker, TJ's the one performing on the advert playing the guitar and singing.

Uncle Jack Dupree holds a future author in his arms

Jim and Nigel Wilson with Champion Jack Dupree outside his home in Halifax.

Apart from Jim's Trad Jazz band in the late 1950s, Jim also managed a Sheffield comedy / pop Group in the Sixties called, *Bob Andrews and the Questors,* that later became the regionally well-known club band, *The Four Blades*. Jim's business cards show them as, *The Four Blades…Four sharp lads from Sheffield….* Graham Palmer said that they had a great following especially when they played the clubs in and around Barnsley.

Bob Andrews and the Questors was fronted by a sixteen-year-old singer called Robert Wass, his stage name being Bob Andrews, later to change again to Bobby Knut. Further on in life Bobby was to become a successful stand-up comedian and theatre and television actor; appearing in shows such as The Last of the Summer Wine, Coronation Street and Emmerdale Farm.

The Questors had put an advert in the newspaper for a man with a van to carry all their equipment, and Jim had answered the advert, being well into playing music himself and having an Atlas three-speed van.

The Four Blades "Four sharp lads from Sheffield" pictured on the stairs of the City Hall. Ascending from left to right: Phil Galley, Graham Palmer, Rodger Bailey and Ken Timms

Backing Bobby was Ken Timms on bass, Phil Galley on drums, Rodger Bailey on lead guitar and Graham Palmer on rhythm guitar and vocals.

When Bobby left the group the band's name changed to, *The Four Blades. The band's name* was a joint decision that they came up with between them, and had nothing to do with football; although Graham, being a Wednesday fan, was not keen on the name; but Graham said he was out voted; realizing and coming to terms to the fact that the band's name referred to where they all came from…at that time, Sheffield was still renowned as the World's Capital of Steel.

Bobby, when on stage, looked a bit like Buddy Holly, with those famous black framed glasses. However, he was likened to Freddie Garrity in Freddie and the Dreamers in the press, who were another comedy pop beat band, but originating from Manchester.

I remember Jim saying that at one point, earlier on in the band's career that he had turned down Joe Cocker…because he already had Bobby.

Jim's words to me and himself were: *"Fancy turning Joe Cocker down!"* and then laughing…so I was never sure if he was joking. And at that time I was too young to care either way. (But looking back on Jim's amazing life, I think it is highly likely to be true…Joe at that time was working for the gas board as a gas fitter with Graham Palmer.)

Jim hand-built Bobby, a number of top-quality cycle frames and bikes over the years, and I remember one time as a young lad being behind the shop counter serving with Jim, when Bobby came in and saw me scratching my nose, and he instantly said to me, *"Stop picking your nose. Your mums just swept up!"*

Ironically, Bobby left the Questors / Four Blades to join another band called the Whirlwinds. Missing out when the Four Blades went touring overseas; later in life Bobby had some regrets that he had left, especially as all the band members were his good friends. Bobby thought Jim was just talking and dreaming about touring with the band at home and abroad, not realising that my father was the kind of man to make friends and contacts in France and anywhere else he went during his war days, and also of course after the war, through his contacts in the sport of cycle racing and the cycle business.

Mum and Dad, enjoying themselves in France, Merlimont. Olive and Jim Wilson were a very special couple, and they shared their happy lives giving love and kindness to everyone.

The Four Blades with Jim as manager, toured with the Milk Race one year, entertaining the crowds at the finish of each stage. Then the band would go to the South of France, playing in the nightclubs and American Army bases. Here being on the verge of a record and radio station deal, until Roger Bailey and Graham Palmer went for a ride in a blue Cadillac (to buy some guitar strings, my mother kindly informs me;) belonging to an American soldier stationed over there at St Nazaire. Unbeknownst to Graham and Roger the GI had been drinking. The end result came on the road to La Baul when the Caddy and company was involved in an RTA. Roger dislocating his shoulder and Graham breaking his back. The G.I. walked away unscathed! Graham recovered over the next 12 months but never returned to the band, the Blades just seemed to fizzle out after that, until there was Ken and Jim left. Ken joined a band to work on the clubs and Jim started playing and singing the blues with Uncle Jack, as one of his Premonitions.

Bobby left the *Whirlwinds*, and formed a comedy duo with their keyboard player, naming themselves *Pea and Knut*, luckily Bob's agent persuaded Bob to go it alone. Later on in life Bobby would write two autobiographical books about his life, and he mentions Jim Wilson and his bike shop in both of them. In Bobby's first book called *Eyup Knutty* (same title as the sequel), there is a picture of Bobby winning a charity bike race on his JF Wilson racing bike that took place on the Isle of Jersey early in the 1980s.

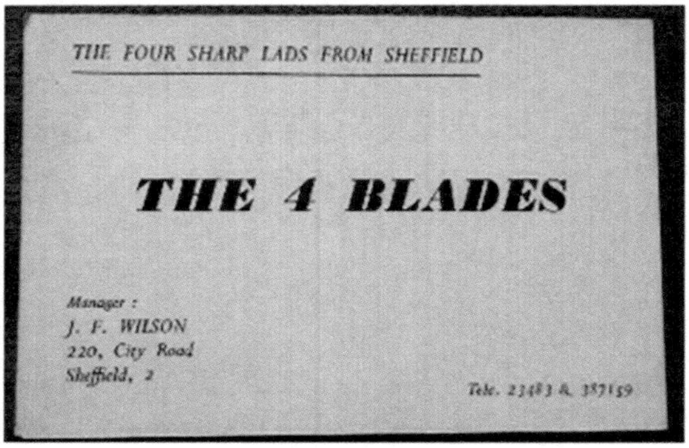

Four Blades Business Card

One day, Peter Stringfellow, then a young night club owner, called Jim on the telephone to see if he would let the Beatles use his Vox amplifier when they came to play in Sheffield just up the road from Jim's bike shop, JF Wilson Cycles on City Road. Of course Jim obliged, as these things sometimes workout, John, Paul, George and Ringo, The Fab Four, could have literally collected the amp from the bike shop on their way to the gig.

KKK

Jim toured around England and Germany with Jack Dupree's band, *THE PREMONITIONS*, and when they were in London, they ended up at a séance.

Jack Dupree's group The Premonitions pictured here in Sheffield City Centre, Virtuoso guitarist Granville Hill far right stands next to Jim. Steve Walker (middle) and Dave Robinson 2nd from reader's left.

It was a fashionable thing to do at the time for bands and a bit of a laugh.

When it came to Jack's turn, the glass slowly went to K…K…K.

Jim said that Jack turned pale!

Throughout his life, Jack had not told a soul, but Jim eventually learnt from Jack that when he was a very young boy, the Ku Klux Klan had murdered his mother and father.

Epilogue

Jim was a quietly-spoken and an unassuming gentleman. And even though only standing six foot, two inches tall, he possessed a presence that I will find hard to put into words. Charismatic would perhaps give the wrong impression, but an indefinable charisma there was. A leader by example would be better. Innovative, with a clever understanding of all things. A natural yogic, and certainly an enlightened man. A profoundly happy person, who could kill you in seconds with one bare hand.

Accurate blue eyes that you would be a fool to call dreamy. And yet playing his Hammond organ and singing a blues song, his eyes and lids did at times give that impression. Cool and laid-back in character. Calm and quiet, like a rock in the river of life. Someone who fitted perfectly into his era, like time itself. Reminiscent in looks, of James Stuart, in those old Alfred Hitchcock films, in particular Christmastime's, *It's a wonderful life....*but with a nerveless Tarzan centre. And a voice, with words that were in their way quiet, (if at all spoken), and yet attained—not necessarily by any higher volume—an expanding welcoming presence in your mind; a language or conversation that at times seemed unspoken, as if you had thought of the words yourself...a loving kind of telepathy. A form of sign language with merely facial signs and feelings, would at times be the only answer to your question.

Jim pictured above wearing his Sheffield Phoenix jersey, raced in the Inaugural Tour of Britain, followed by the next three Tours of Britain, and had numerous placings aboard in Semi-Classics, e.g. sixth place Hanover-Brunswick and rides and *finishes* in Classics such as the Tour of Flanders. Compared to the palmeres of today's top riders, they may not sound such a big deal, but at this time you had to do it all yourself, and Jim was thirty two years old now, not twenty years of age, and as previously mentioned, his best years physically were spent during the Second World War. And the post war years were about trying to recover something approaching normal health…which for Jim did not mean careful, self-pampering, it meant action. There was no one to take you by the hand and carry you round. And instead of EPO, it was bread and jam, and a '*hang a man once, hang him again; he'll get used to it'* attitude. A golden courageousness that the souped-up glamour puppies of the future would never dream of, let alone attain…thanks in part to the modern media, its big money business, and the follow on corrupt sporting political system that it generates.

*

Jim was a highly successful team manager, and he found sponsorships such as Ovaltine, Alp, Airlite, Benelux, Tizer (BARR), Hi-Lift, Dare Grips, O'Brien, Singer (sewing machines) and more…to create and run various winning teams, one of which, aside from the Wilson Cycles team, was the *Elswick Hopper* Team in 1958.

In short Jim Wilson was an amazing bike rider, athlete and person, considering he had come back from near fatal injuries after being left to fend for himself on the beaches at Dunkirk. These feats proved to be a Great Inspiration to many other people at that time, and they still do—to those who care to know—today!

My father's greatest talent was bringing people together from all walks of life, and selflessly making them into something greater than they may have realised, being left to themselves and society.

Jim Wilson was a very stylish rider, not dissimilar to a Stephen Roche

Jim, not only being a Royal Engineer, was also a stylish cycle frame builder and a practical innovator and using these skills and gifts he put them to great use in improving function and design in cycle frame building. He was the first (in the UK at least if not Europe!) during the 1950s to introduce rear wheel frame dropouts with a gear hanger onto his frames: Cutting the rear derailleur hangers off of the rear gear and brazing them directly onto the frame's rear dropouts. Also moving on a decade into the 1960s Jim was possibly the first frame builder to put seat stays onto a plate at the back of the seat tube at various positions, a style that we termed as *'Fast Back'* seat stays. Later on, more commonly known as shot-in seat stays, and usually, by this time, shot directly into the seat bolt at the top of the seat tube.

This was a move away from the wrap round seat stays, and added a sleeker *JF Wilson* hallmark, to Jim's already individualistic cycle frames; a style that has been imitated for many years. And always will be...if it's already right...why try to reinvent the circle?

But the media and their throwaway industries will always tamper with perfections to sell you something 'different' that isn't as good and hence disposable...to constantly relieve fools of their money. The industry of the modern media have made crapness fashionable. And here is a poem that I wrote around the year 2000, to mark out this appalling fact; it was inspired by this worldwide, sorry sea change, and it is appropriately called:

"The Industrial Ruin of the Word Quality"

Sheffield made Steel and was World renowned,
And then when the media world and Taiwan "regurgitated" alloy and now Car-bonfire-fibre, we found,
Strong and very good exchanged for expensively cheap, convenient dud.
Future usefulness sold off, un-noticed in our present day consumer rush,
Encroaching crumbling letdown, forgiven by expected, forgotten by acceptance.

Tat! Disguised as quality in modern day media sheen,
Imitated memories of the craftsman.
That was not just a dream!

During the mid-1970s, a young, up and coming cyclo-cross star of the future, Chris Ledger, was out on a Sheffield Phoenix club run with Jim. They had stopped off near Worksop, at the little airport that had a café, and Chris was amazed, when Jim started playing on the piano (very well) that they happened to have inside the cafe; but there was more astonishment to come, when Jim mentioned to Chris that he had just signed Hennie Kuiper and Franceso Moser at a cycle show. The story goes that Kuiper had switched the bunch at the end of the amateur World Road Race Championships that year, and was in hot water with various federations, governing bodies and riders. Hennie was obviously keeping his options open! Moser's is another story; and while Chris reminds me of these two outstanding riders, so is Germany's Klaus Peter Thaler.

Not many British teams could ever boast of such names on their roster. And remember at this time, these riders had not yet reached their full potential! Had Britain been more of an open SPORTING Nation, I guarantee that Jim would have easily found the bigger sponsors to hold on to these riders.

So Long! Auf Wiedersehen!

Jim belonged to a unique generation, where there was many a helpful soul, as if they appreciated other people's lives as their own. Maybe this was one of those rare silver linings to gleam out of World War II. It made those involved, who had survived, respect everyone's aspect in life. As though they might not be there together tomorrow.

Jim was cool and calculating like Roche but tough as a Kelly with the heart of a lion, or a Merckx.

Today a lot more people know about cancer through the media; (In my opinion, that is when the media is at its best…Please see *'Wash Your Own Brain'* in my second book *Straining Your Psyche Through the Veil*) and thankfully, we have become educated to be aware of the signs and catch it in time, to have a better chance of survival. For years, when Jim was in a lot of pain, we always put it down to his 'war wound', not prostrate and bowel cancer! And still, half a century on, I have never met a person since, with so much quiet, patient, happy inspiring drive, sheer love for life and all the people in it.

Jim riding a Dursley Pederson cycle, courtesy of Roy Barrett. Photo taken circa 1978

Jim Wilson, still racing at 39 years of age alongside his brother Syd Wilson, aged 29, to the reader's right

Look at how many trophies Jim's cycle racing team won in one year

Close up of Jim's Tour of Britain plaque. One of 4

The oldest rider in the race, Jim Wilson, 39 years old, team leader and sponsor, climbs Red Hill near Great Harrowden, on the first lap of the Grand Prix of Wellingborough, 14th September 1958.

The Sport of Cycle racing was Jim's number one love

During a stage in the Tour of Britain, a rider put his pedal into Jim's rear wheel and buckled it to such an extent that the rim was hitting the break blocks hard, and some of the spokes that had snapped stuck outwards at nearly 90 degrees, so they slapped the seat and chain stays of his frame on every revolution of the wheel. I asked, "What did you do?" Jim simply said, *"I rode harder!"*

Eventually the spokes broke off and Jim finished the stage.

Then and Now

1950s newspaper shot of Jim Wilson and his craftsmanship near the doorway of his shop at 220 City Road, Sheffield. The legacy continues, to this day

Super road race sprinter Ron Coe was a prolific winner for J.F. Wilson Cycles, and his favorite bike was a fully chromed J.F. Wilson

The author within his father's shop. Proudly displaying Jim's poster and his Tour of Britain trophies. Along with Nigel's first, hand-built 531 frame that Jim built for him when he was 5 years old. The little frame is now a very special heirloom

Jim Wilson outside his shop at 220 City Road with Martin Harpham and National Road Race Champion Roy Hempsall. Note, at first, I thought that there were net curtains in the shop window, but Jim had made a friend of a shop window dresser who was a fan of the shop and Jim's exploits in cycling

Part of the Wilson Cycles racing team: From left to right: John Bennett, Doug Petty, Dave Orford, Ken Strattford, Syd Wilson and Jim Wilson. Photo taken at Low Bradfield (Dam Flask) near Sheffield circa mid 1950s

Jim Wilson's Number 1 Fan, his wife Olive Wilson, seen here far left, with my aunty Sybil right, sat on the bumper of a Ford V8 Pilot automobile, and J.F.WILSON CYCLES TEAM car.

Jim with team helper and yet another sponsor on the Wilson Team Car

In one Tour of Britain stage, Jim had broken away alone about halfway through a stage, when with 15 miles to go his left hand pedal came off, and Jim had to ride with one leg to the finish, only to be caught by a group of riders with around 200 yards to go to the finish line… note my father is carrying the pedal, toe-clip and strap in his hand; very little went to waste that could be saved in this era.

.47

ms.
45
71
44
49
:02

59
75
:02
51
51
31
41½
:00
85

3S

lessin
178).
1134)
).
enis*
raus*
500).
308),
480),
sque*
k are
venir.

ALTHOUGH the British selections for the made very early, there have been sev names were released. These were the two to press.

TOUR de FRANCE

TOM SIMPSON (Rapha-Gitane).
BRIAN ROBINSON (Gem.-St. Raphael)
SHAY ELLIOTT (Helyett-Fyn).
RON COE (Wilson Cycles).
VIN DENSON (Temple Cycles).
ALBERT HITCHEN (Viking Cycles).
ALF HOWLING (Rapha-Gitane).
GEORGE O'BRIEN (Viking Cycles).
KEN LAIDLAW.
SEAN RYAN (Henry Holmes Cycles).
STAN BRITTAIN (Viking Cycles).
IAN MOORE (Liberia Grammont).
Manager: SAUVEUR DUCAZEAUX.
Masseurs: J. PROVOST
W. SHILLIBEER.
Mechanics: A. BUTTLER
N. ROBERTS.

T
BILL BI
HUGH
JIM HI
ALAN .
GORDO
ALAN
ALAN
MEL D.
Manage
Masseu
Mechai

On the
explair
re

Written proof that Jim Wilson put riders in the Tour De France riding for his shop Wilson Cycles, a small terraced house on City Road in Sheffield, a feat that has never been done before and never will be achieved again throughout the history of the Tour De France.

Jim Wilson, building a J.F. Wilson frame in Reynolds 531 tubing

German Tour of Rheinland Pfalz

A Team win in the German Tour of the Rheinland Pfalz, with Jim Wilson as Team Manager in the Autumn of his career. From left to right: Brian Pownall, John Kenworthy (Stage Winner), Colin Thornton and Roy Taylor.

GB Team Manager, Jim Wilson at the Start of the 1975 German Tour of the Rheinland Pfalz

The 1975 Tour of Rheinland was remembered for its boiling hot weather. Roy Taylor, pictured left said "It was the first time I discovered that descending mountains in the Rhine Valley you actually got hotter, as they retained the heat." Roy collapsed with heat exhaustion 200 metres from the finish of one stage and was encouraged to get up and walk to the line by Jim and his mechanic. Here, Jim with young fans gives Roy some 4 star water.

Great Britain Team Manager Jim Wilson, 2nd right at the German Tour of the Rheinland Pflaz: with from left to right Mick Wishart, Colin Thornton, John Kenworthy (Oldham Century top) Roy Taylor (sitting down) and Brian Pownall.

Other Books by the Same Author:

Stories For All The Children Of All The Worlds
Straining Your Psyche Through the Veil
Sam the Super Powered Musical Moon